Spirit of Place

Spirit of Place

Mendocino County
Women Poets Anthology

*Edited by Devreaux Baker, Maureen Eppstein, Karen Lewis,
Kate Dougherty, blake more and Georgina Marie Guardado*

WAYFIND PRESS

Library of Congress Control Number: 2025901039
Printed in the United States of America
ISBN:979-8-9913652-0-8

Published by Wayfind Press
Mendocino, CA
e-mail: dbaker@mcn.org
www.devreauxbaker.org

Cover art and design: Solange Roberdeau
Interior design: Maureen Eppstein
Font: Garamond

Produced for on-demand distribution by Ingram/Lightning Source for Wayfind Press

*To know who you are, you have to have
a place to come from.*

— Carson McCullers

Contents

Foreword

Mendocino County is a very diverse region and is home to a variety of writers. Many of these writers are poets, some of whom write under the radar, penning or tapping the keyboards in distant hamlets throughout this unique region and who are showcased in *Spirit of Place: Mendocino County Women Poets Anthology*. This publication, sister to the 1999 anthology *Wood, Water, Air and Fire*, offers views of that diversity and women whose voices come off the page speaking of this beautiful and rugged landscape, and the lives they've experienced residing here.

Growing up in Mendocino County, exposure to poetry was limited to certain English classes showcasing the classics: Poe, Whitman, Frost, etc. As the region grew and experienced the height and collapse of both the logging and marijuana industries, the coming of the back-to-landers, the women's movement, and environmental awareness, so grew the presence of poetry.

Publications such as the *Coast Peddler, Outlook* and *New Settler Review* not only offered pages dedicated to poetry but showcased the lives of writers. California Poets in the Schools taught in even the most rural areas, small open mic nights occurred, and a poetry community blossomed encompassing the county.

All those efforts led to publications such as *Spirit of Place,* offering women writers the opportunity to share their individual views. The editors have garnered pieces that illustrate the region's natural beauty, while delving deeper into what Mendocino County means to those who are life-long residents and others, who came for the beauty or sometimes personal and random reasons and stayed. The collection includes well-established poets whose poems were in the early *Wood, Water, Air and Fire* Anthology as well as new and upcoming writers who have never been published.

Enjoy the view.

—.Linda Noel
Poet Laureate Emerita, Willits
Koyungkowi Tribe

xi

Preface

For several years I have carried the phrase, 'spirit of place' with me. When I felt overwhelmed by the on-going crises in the world, that phrase brought me a sense of peace and helped me find the time and space to reflect on my relationship with the land. For me this relationship is a reciprocal one with my environment. As a poet I used the phrase to inspire and refresh my own writing and, in that way, also used it as a kind of light in the dark. It helped me gain a sense of calm in what otherwise felt like a storm of uncertainty.

It was during those moments that I also reflected on the power of community as support and inspiration for its poets. Mendocino has long been a mecca for poets and has provided a haven for new poets to share their work. When I think of engaging with Mendocino County as inspiration for creating poetry, I imagine a relationship with the environment occurring filled with many diverse elements from redwoods, pygmy forests or coastal beaches to eclectic conversations of small-town importance held in grocery store lines or post offices stretching from Point Arena, Elk, Mendocino, Fort Bragg, and Westport, to Ukiah, Willits and Covelo.

M.L. Harrison Mackie published the first anthology of Mendocino Women Poets; *Wood, Water, Air and Fire*, with Pot Shard Press in Comptche, California in 1998. I was one of three editors on that book and was struck by the many diverse women poets living and working and committed to writing poetry in Mendocino. Twenty-seven years later it seemed important to me to once again invite women poets to contribute to a book of poetry.

This time I wanted to include women poets not just from Mendocino but from the entire county. I wanted to use the phrase 'spirit of place' as a touchstone and title for this book and ask women to submit poems that reflected in some way what that phrase meant to them, and their own relationships with the environment of Mendocino County. I was fortunate to work with five talented editors who were instrumental in helping to shape and bring the initial vision of an anthology of voices into completion: Maureen Eppstein, Karen Lewis, Kate Dougherty, blake more, and Georgina Marie Guardado.

For me, the importance of poetry goes far beyond the power or beauty of individual poems. Poetry belongs to the world and although it might begin as an isolated act of creation, it comes to fruition in community. In Mendocino County we are lucky to be able to say we have a huge population of poets. We have communities of poets both coastal and inland hosting readings, sharing poetry in the schools, or reading poetry with local gatherings of friends in private homes, cafes, hotels and bars. Today I find that rather miraculous.

When I think of 'spirit of place' I think of 'archeology of place' creating a 'footprint' that lives in the past, present and future interactions of people with the land they inhabit. I think in terms of memories, hopes, dreams and stories passed down through generations that form a vast living tapestry and can inspire, guide and shape our lives and the life of the planet.

It is not lost on me that I live on land where native people were massacred, enslaved and forcibly removed and that this too is energy that resides in the landscape. I carry deep respect and awareness of all the native peoples whose lives were forever changed by the history of settler abuse.

Finally, I believe in the power of poems to re-connect the disconnected, so in that way it becomes a bridge of communication between people who live spread out in a county that is largely rural. It is my hope that *Spirit of Place: Mendocino County Women Poets Anthology* will continue to add to that bridge of connection and I am honored and excited to be a part of the process of bridge-building that poetry, in the best of all possible worlds, affords us all; to give a voice to the voiceless, to illuminate what is hidden, to surprise the jaded, to encourage the individuals who write their poems in secret to share their words with others, and to perhaps in some small way help heal the world.

— Devreaux Baker
Mendocino County Poet Laureate

Water

Karen Kellam

Shoreline
Point Arena, 1970's

From the wild coast across the highway
seals barked us awake at dawn.
We collected driftwood for fire.
I made bread. The artichokes you
planted grew large, their hearts nestled
in spiky purples and turtle belly greens.

A returning sparrow hawk perched
on our swing set eyeing the scratchy lawn.
I remember us younger and strong
not exactly carefree, our children
beautiful and full of joy
and the need of us.

Shallow roots of tall redwoods
stretched centuries in fog-saturated earth.
Deer grazed on the high bluffs
and orange poppies dazzled through
a maze of spring iris.

Once, as though in a dream—
a doe slipped from the cliff
and rode helpless on the waves.
Starfish clung to craggy rocks
bonded in a surge of water on stone—
stone abrading into sand.

And now weathered in age I feel
the lull of on-shore breezes
fiery sunsets and plummeting
cormorants when the sights and sounds
of sea, our pacific shoreline, meant home.

Lauren Oertel

Ascending the Staircase

In this corner of emerald coastline
landscape evolution painted
through marine terrace sequences
haunts the shared story.

Groans of the Pacific saturate
the air. Waves crash on sea stacks
followed by the whisper of the water receding.
Shorelines and sea levels rise,
absorb the melt of continental glaciers.
Retreating waves spread gravel and sand
coastal gusts deposit beach material.
All of this building and tearing away
rebuilding then shattering,
reveals hidden layers beneath.

Savannah Sparrows with their buzzy songs
forage through bluff grasslands
weave nests in ground depressions
knowing their young will leave
soon after hatching.
They return to this home each year.

Flinch with the touch of Sitka spruce needles
piney citrus mist dusts the atmosphere.
Douglas squirrels devour seeds,
tunnel homes into mounds of cone remnants.
With shallow roots, spruce crash, leveled by gusts.
Absence creates gaps
of light for the ginseng-scented
Devils club, potent healer.

More gusts, more shifts, and waves.
Climb the ecological staircase
into the Pygmy Forest,
this beacon of resilience
glows in its survival.

4

C Rowan Hawthorn

Here

The coastline is a dream
a rendering of what
a coastline should be
I have to avert my eyes from
the fairy realm effect
of the water
for, when I look at it
I succumb to
rocky shore thoughts
to blue water reveries
to something that
visits me in sleep
Raven wing flights
over white foam disintegrations
Here
there is no Time
I am the sea
the fog
the sky
Here
I am not awake
Here
I fall away
and the coastline dreams
of itself

Sharon Doubiago

Pacific Ocean Breaks, My Poetics

> *for my surfer son Danny who gave me the word, bioluminescences,*
> *for my daughter, Shawn, who gave us my grandson, Ryan.*

they come in   from every direction   no knowing
which way they'll turn   break
so wild   foamy in excess their beauty even before
they crash   so monstrously huge   their lust   their light

upon the sand   upon each other   breath
taking   from where on earth
did this come   sometimes
disappointing   piddly   you

turn away   but they don't
stop   wave
upon wave plowing in   so conflicting
their path   so contrary
the silver soaked shore

going south now   head ripped off
flying behind   the next   tunnel
too immense   a girl drowning   in the rip tide   nothing

makes her feel more at home seeing them coming   nothing
makes her more the poet than these long silver lines
coming in

and going back

exploding their own order   all
civil orders   the churning

mudgold blue of the terrorist undertow in front
slanting off   the opposite way   the one behind colliding   they
never stop   too many they don't sum up   the light
writing the universe   the bioluminescences
of autumn   the girl's neon body

face down in the sand
gasping for air   pound and roar   ever changing rhythm

moan of earth   turning over
to the blinding suneye

star surf   of heaven   her
son and daughter inside   surfing to shore

Nancy Wallace Nelson

Angled for Survival

the stark white surf
breaks exuberant on the rocks
surrounded by cobalt sea.
jagged twists of rock
outline the shore moving north
in startling brilliance.
terns, gulls and crows
dance above me
floating on the currents.
the cypress trunks
are wise and bent low,
turning away from the cliffs,
seeking refuge
from fierce, relentless winds.
hunkered toward the ground
dug into the soil, the trees survive.
and isn't that the stance I need?
aging in place
here in my woods
angled for survival.

Henri Bensussen

Alternate Planes (Jug Handle, September)

Crumbling bluffs above a withdrawn, low-tide Pacific,
reefs, seamounts, resident life bared to heat, hungry
gulls. We gaze at what the ocean opens up for us. Jez
isn't lingering for artful shots of nature's hideouts.

She wants time: to complete the Pacific Coast Trail
(this was the year I planned to do it), and her garden—
more white and blue, with dots of pure yellow
(no orange, no blaring red). A deep black flower would

Background all that white, to mirror what she's
wrestled with for weeks since pain & scans proclaimed
a thing growing on her liver, stretching now to spleen.
Neither surgery nor any treatment relevant: No guarantees.

Lifts her ribs, thumbing the skin, she says, I push it out
of the way so I can sleep. Two more years: to see young
cherries bloom white against white paths, beds of white
roses, Shasta daisies, blue bachelor's buttons. Should I

plant annuals or perennials? A serious question: Oscar
Wilde heroine bemoaning a fate she expects he will
shield her from in the final act. High stakes gamble
with death, a refusal to accept that Wilde's long gone.

We stare at a glistening view of bright green sea grass
languishing among the tidal currents, latched to rock
by roots defying waves marching in from a far continent.

I'm still transfixed by that water world when Jez says,
The body dies, but one might enter some alternate plane.
She plunges on past sword fern, ravaged pines, over-ripe
mushrooms, me dripping salt and intent on catching up,
path opening to a field of drying grass the color of straw.

Mary Rice

Blowhole to Punchbowl

Curious blood-red bluff squirrel
Looking directly up at me

Wind driven relentless waves
Heard meeting distant shores
Rocks on fire
Sunset ushering in crimson petticoats
Like forgotten missing indigenous women

Salty waves in my eyes
Searching
For solace - a resting place
Each wave rekindles my grief
It is said some have died here, an elegiac prequel

The punchbowl before me
Has opened its mouth
Calling

Galump-ga-BOOM
And echo

Revealing secrets below
Has someone heard its call

At the rim of the punchbowl
Blackberries now dormant
Projecting bare sharp thorns
A warning
Point to the gaping jaws, ready to catch a falling star

Below
Between sea, earth and
Beyond

Gargantuan meat grinder
Cement mixer

Thrashes, pulverizes

Galump-ga-BOOM
And echo

Light bursting through punchbowl's ancient eye
Looking directly up at me

Devreaux Baker

Big River Adagio

Twilight at Big River beach and pelicans are circling tidal pools
searching for a safe place to drift and dream in the coming dark.

Anxious to empty the day's thoughts and leave them as footprints
to be washed out to sea, I walk barefoot on the sand. The light is filled

with that soft familiar voice that acts as intermediary between night
            and day
but I feel the old sorrow for no reason that rises and falls in sea wind

and seems to permeate the air and belong to this rocky shore and in
            belonging
to the shore also belongs to me. I think of the family of all of us
            walking together

like this through twilight, opening some long-lost book of the dead
            trying
to make sense of the senseless puzzle that is the violent history that
            permeates

our lives, until all the diverse pieces of that puzzle are drawn to fit
            themselves
back together and abide with this other uncanny feeling of something
            forever lost

or disappearing all around us. It is the lay of the storm-washed rocks
            at the edge
of the cliffs that offer solace in their abiding grace on the margins of
            water and land

that can suddenly bring me to my knees and remind me there is still
            time
to be a part of the cartography of surprising possibilities in this
            lowering dark.

I can sit awhile and allow the voices from the past and present to
            create a tapestry

of lives that offer comfort in this cold Pacific air and perhaps like the
        pelicans,

seek a haven, quiet my questions of why or what for, by drifting into
        the space
that time offers, in the folds of her dark blue tent.

Zomala Abell

The River Mouth

here where the sea comes in

and the river flows out

the sky touches the sand

and I am so tiny in my boots

so vague in my thoughts

even my gratitude sifts through my fingers.

here where the sea breathes

and the smaller river waves

lap their way to freedom

my own breath empties

and my body fills with light.

here where the sea comes in

and the river flows out

only the silence of the stillness within

is louder than the hungry roar

of the tides.

Maureen Eppstein

What Matters
For JH

That on a morning the color of oyster shell
the grassy riverbank
lies mirrored in the glassy flow.

As the river touches the sea
we touch to make meaning.

If I had nothing, the poet said
not keyboard nor pen nor paper
I would write with a stick in the sand

though tides wash the marks away,
because this is what I must do.

Beyond the river a sand spit
littered with driftwood.
Sea foam lifts.

Wave caresses sand
like a child the head of a favorite dog.
A gull circles and cries.

Hand imagines roundness of stick.
What matters is the making.

Susan Schaefer Bernardo

Rock and Water

I am water, and he is rock.
Ours is an ancient attraction
of seeming opposites,
a complicated marriage.
We come together in many places, waltzing dreamily
amid limestone pillars and chandeliers in dazzling underground
                caverns,
or marveling at each other's crystalline structures on snowy peaks.
Sometimes, I spring up to surprise him in his quiet retreats –
he faithfully lifts me high into the sky
with a belly laugh of heat.
We have our struggles – what lovers don't?
Heaven knows, he has his faults, and I can be shallow.
I like to have my way, and when he is slow to find his,
I impatiently trickle down the face of his towering monolith
wedge myself there in tight cold places, shivering,
my ice expanding against his granite, decomposing him a bit
so that eagle-borne seeds can take root and soften him further.
When he falls headlong from the heights, I pick him up and tumble
                him along,
smoothing and polishing his jagged edges until we gleam together in
                the sunlight.
Sometimes when he's had his fill of me,
he deserts me for his dusty cave, dwelling there
with spined and scaled creatures, which struggle to survive without me.
Hot, bothered by his resistance, I storm away, high into the clouds,
until at last he relents with a sigh of sand, and I
pour down upon him, a flash flood of desire,
merging us into mud, making him my own again, carving ravines which
snake across the desert floor, quenching the barren landscape
until it explodes with brilliant color.
Our favorite rendezvous is the intertidal zone,
where we meet to dance morning and night.
I hurtle myself forward as he stands solemnly at the edge
and he catches me, strong and hard, spins me high with a swirl of
                foam,
a Spanish dancer flourishing my petticoats of lacy white.

Laughing, I cling to him before I flow down his side and back out to
        sea.
I race forward again and again, higher and higher,
until he is submerged beneath me.
The tender things that take refuge in his hollow places,
protected by sturdy shells and a wet blanket,
come out to play with us then –
the sea anemones open like exotic flowers,
mussels extend delicate tongues to sip the rich brine,
a hermit crab makes itself vulnerable, scurrying across our sea bed
toward a larger shell home, and the brittle sea stars tangle themselves
into their exuberant tango and we feel joy fully.
I sing him a love song I learned from the whales,
my voice rippling the golden forest of kelp that holds fast to him
        below.
He tells me the riddles he has learned from the sun and wind
and the winged things that ride between them.
But all too soon mother moon tells me it is time to go
I lap tenderly at his feet a few moments more,
then reluctantly pull away to my deep self.
Soon I am cresting with the dolphins, rejoicing in the currents
which take me to distant shores, plunging my own depths and
        maelstroms
until I become dizzy with them and find myself alone in the dark,
blinded by phosphorescent lures
feeling bottomless, and so cold
until he touches me there in the deep, and I remember that he is here,
everywhere, supporting me, moving me,
providing the heat flowing up and through me,
that he is liquid like me at the core,
a magnanimous molten river, erupting and cooling to form new land
where we can dance once more at the edges between us.

Lorna Rauscher

Oceans of Love

Sunlight danced across the ocean,
Two lovers walked hand in hand.
Nature's wonders so magnificent
Leaving shells strewn through sand.
Their hearts so young and innocent,
Discovering life so fresh and new.
As waves came crashing forth,
Tickling toes with soft white foam
Such days like this were few.
We have each other was all they thought,
With happiness and carefree times too.
Footprints made on the path they walk,
Words of love they would softly talk.
Let us always come back to the sea,
The sounds, the smells, the beauty,
That will always surround you and me.

Janice Marcell

Visiting Noyo River in the Summertime

we confidently ignore the No Trespassing signs
posted by our mother for the public
and forge onward, along the forest path leading to the Noyo River

as children we just slid down the side of a cliff
our path was ruggedly measured
by our repetitive excursions

today we must use the somewhat worn redwood forest path
it only leads in one direction
downward, towards the forest green river

now there's a rocky stream to traverse
caused by multiple prominent hillside springs
we gingerly step on the stones that hold our weight well

carefully we descend through the grove of stinging nettles
then further down across the logging road
that outlines the inviting water

my brothers run ahead to the wooden bridge
they earnestly cast their fishing lines into the cool water
as I meditate on the beauty of this magnificent place

Linda Noel

Night River

She sat on the edge of his firm bed
　　The midnight hour several blinks away
　　　　His breathing, her silence
　　　　　　　The digital clock hum and glow

She fears he or the silence might ask why
　　　　Why are you going, why can't you stay?
She searches short and quick to cock her response
　　　　She searches for her sock
He says nothing and breathes deeply
　　　　She feels each breath calling her back
　　　　　　His fingers reach her spine before he speaks
　　　　　　　　Into thick darkness

You have too much love to contain
　　　　　　Too much heart to keep to yourself
　　　So why
　　　　　　Hide?

She trembles knowing that every nerve ending in
　　　　　His each finger tip feels her backbone shaking
　　　　　　　　As his words fall off North Bay air

It is neither foreplay nor the ember of after glow

His fingers recede into palm, into arm, into his own heart
　　　　　And she summons the courage to breathe
　　　　　　　　These words into sound

　　　　　　　My love is a wild river
　　　　　　　It can be brutal and beautiful

　　　　　　My love is a wild river
　　　　　　　Green and inviting, muddy and unrelenting

And within the blink he replies
　　　　　　So do you want to drown in it to remain

20

Affirmed in your independence and self-reliance?

His words both ambush and dazzle her
    They have been well considered
        She is frightened she must flee
            She puts her lips on his one more time
                He knows the chances of her returning are
                    As slim as the road leading from his house

It was an after midnight flight, escape from her own heart
                              Pulse of truth
        She knows this as she slopes onto the freeway north
           To a cooler and shadowy country she cries to stars
              Who listen and leave their own moisture as proof
                            Of night
A night-given song about the color of a salmon's heart
        When it is carried as burden and stored in a worn
           Willow basket held between the blades of her shoulders

She speaks her thanks as night deepens
                And comforts the journey home

Karin Faulkner

Rain On The River

Ssshhhh she's gone, she died sssshhhhh
She's dead sshhhh she's -
Raindrops fall on the quiet river
Ripples ripples ripples surround each drop
Squint your eyes, they become teardrops
Squint more, hearts expand and spread
Like charms on a bracelet
across the river's arm

Hearts almost meeting on the skin dividing
Air from water each in its own slow current
Almost bridging life and death
Here where everything flies floats swims or drowns

Squint and relax your eyes again
Ripples become lily pads transparent glisten-edged still
Still just able to bear the weight
Of one soul

'Gate' gate' para gate' parasumgate' bodhi svaha'
Gone gone beyond, fully beyond.
Oh, such awakening ! Hail the traveler.'

Ssssh ssshh she is gone into Silence I chanted into silence
I chanted through silence the Gate' Gate' I chanted chanted
For her passage

Here at the drizzly soft river, my eyes only Buddha-opened
I clearly hear the fairy tip tips sip sips, the meetings of falling drops
With their endless endless home
Direct union. Were they individual drops a moment ago?
Are they individual drops now?
Like light welcoming a traveling soul home.

Kristan M. Larsen

Scattered

Your bones marry with the sea.
Married, you two,
again now as dust and salt.
Sun shining us back up the muddy hill
the powder coats my fingers.
Carrying you on me, with me, of me
my bones made of yours
while your fine silt sits on my skin.
Now the first tears shed
in my new home are not of loneliness,
but of your DNA torn from my soul.
An absence unknowable.
My throat aches for what I can't understand.
So I leave you at the sea
where you belong.

**Thoughts while a man was drowning in the ocean
(and was then found and dragged to shore, but died).**

Please let him live. Please let him live. Please let him. They're so fit.

They must be surfers. Why don't they wear booties. Their feet
are cold, the rocks are too sharp.

Their faces say a life or death situation.

Do they care like this because this is their job? Or is this their job
            because they care like this?

He's probably dead by now.

Why is he naked?
Is he naked because the surf tore off his clothes?
         Is he naked because he took his clothes off to swim
         better? Poor man, his terror.
Poor man, his fear.
Is he naked because he took his clothes off
before he jumped?
         Did he want to become pure?

The way his legs sway in the shallow surf. Like seaweed, the same
         peaceful motion.

If we didn't know better, this would be soothing.

Or,

if we knew better, this would be soothing.

They all know the CPR by heart.
That's their job.
It's too late. Miracles happen. This isn't a movie.

All of us watching are alive.
One of us is dead.

Why don't we talk to each other? Why don't we look at each other?
What is wrong.
What do we feel?

If I could cry, I would be more alive.
If I could cry, I would appear more alive.
Why is no one crying?

She's young, that's why. I want to see her without her mask. I should
hug her.

We are all alive
and one of us is dead.

Thank you thank you thank you thank you

Georgina Marie Guardado

seaside obituary

i remember it exactly as the day it was: gray, overcast, the air salty from pounding waves the coastal winds learned to master. to get there, you had to enter a winding road where either side of the concrete pathway was lined with standing gods in the shapes of redwoods. the scent of the air pungent with pine and petrichor as it entered the pickup truck windows, rolled down just enough to feel the chill. i was his daughter, once. this day may have been the last day it was apparent.

a drive to the ocean side, a walk through old settlement grounds of Jenner, place of original windmills, place of migration. he bought me an abalone hair clip. he ripped seaweed from rocks to humor his daughter, to feed his grumbling hunter stomach. how I long to remember how gentle this day was; how softly he tore the long, dirty green leaves from rugged rocks contrasting how often his hands and words hit harder than the ocean hits sea stacks that have existed long before the sand we once stood on ever contained memory.

how strange, what is revealed when remembrance chooses to reveal itself to you. how a sense of loneliness becomes an unraveling tide controlled not by the moon but by memory that pushes and pulls, opening neurological seascapes of muted recollections that still call my name. the ocean will always outlive us. I have outlived him.

Damieka Thomas

Ocean Poem

I don't believe in ghosts.
But on my way into town,
I saw a man in a pickup just like yours, painted a brilliant red.
He wore a cap with a Harley Davidson logo,
and like you, he had a low ponytail, wispy blonde hair grazing his neck
        like a halo.
He waved at me, and I had to pull over to catch my gasping breath.

Now I watch the ocean moving slowly, the water brushing the shore
like a lover's gentle fingertips grazing skin.
I'm sitting on the beach where you used to take me,
and I'm thinking of your fingertips grazing my baby hairs.
I cannot tell where the sky ends and the ocean begins.

I cannot extract the blue of your eyes from the blue of the ocean.
I cannot forget the way that your voice sounded when you got sick.
Raspy and half-there, like your consciousness.
Damn, you said in one of our last conversations. *You're busy.*
Your guttural voice choked on the syllables.

I cannot forget that the day before you died, I was too busy to call
        back.
I cannot extract my fingertips from the last voicemail you left me,
replaying over and over again like a soft melody whispered into the
        curtain of my hair.
I cannot forgive myself for never calling back.
I cannot understand the way that the sky has swallowed you whole.

I drive home, and I tell my sister about the man in the pickup truck.
Weird, she says. *I saw a man in a red pickup truck waving at me the other day.*
I don't believe in ghosts. I only believe in your seafoam eyes and
        hands like open shores.

Sondra Sula

First Time

The first time I saw a whale breach
was at the Jug Handle headlands.
The day was blustery,
but rain held back,
clutching gray cloud pillows instead.
My destination: The Point
where,
if I were a fly,
I could see three-hundred horizontal degrees of water,
but being me,
stared straight west,
cheating with my peripheral vision.

I suddenly heard a squeal and spun around.
Two very young girls
in colorful chintz floral raincoats
had plopped down on the grass
with their mother in tow.
All three pointed to a spot in the sea
that had been behind my peripheral vision at The Point.

In response to my quizzical look:
"A whale," they giggled, "just jumped!"
How did I miss it? I wondered,
my eyes following their fingertips.
Where they were pointing was too close for a whale,
wasn't it?

And then I saw the massive gray head emerge,
shoot up until only his tail was submerged,
and belly-flop down: smack!
Air rushed into my lungs,
then pushed out a squeal of my own.
The bulky head and smooth body
breached up and slapped down four more times.

We were transfixed.

The event was a first for all of us, I learned.
For the mother,
six years of watching and hoping;
for the children, their entire lives.
For me?
Well, I was lucky.
First time, first time.

Diane Semans

Come See Me

Come see me
I am a killer whale
The largest in the world.

Suspended in the air,
My mighty jaw open
Exposing gigantic teeth.

Come see me
An Alaskan transient
Washed up on your shore.

My fluke
Tangled on a crab pot line,
Six harbor seals in my belly.

Come see me
My flesh now gone
My bones articulated.

Come see me
In all my glory.

Mary Rose Kaczorowski

Seduction

The Navarro River beckons,
She calls for your graceful presence.
Her silky waters flow around your ankles.
Walk slowly. Salmon are singing to you.

Joycelyn Trigg

This

Not that.

Not everything else
lost, left, veiled.

This is the day.

The hard descent to the wild
beach, where driftwood gathers itself,
and kelp, among low waves stroking dark sand.

A quiet breeze tucks the shawl
around us as we sit, watching the sun
smooth sea and sky.

Then, a shining black circle on the water,
growing eyes, a head, a thick glazed back,
a thicker body breaking water

like shackles, like Houdini.
Like a river no dam can hold.

Like the first of us emerging
to find her footing on solid if shifting ground.

Her awkward shuffling, this seal laboring
to the dry sand spread like a rug
at our feet for this birthing.

Like each of us, born
of water. My mother. Hers. Me.

All words lost, and breath, stunned by wonder
that already did not need us
to fill the world.
But maybe it is just
for such a time we have come

to bear witness to this,
and that.

Harriet Gleeson

Charmed Circuit

Quarter-mile on redwood feathers
faintly heard the ocean's roar.
Rain will bring fantastic fungi
coral, brain and dead-man's-foot.
Green translucence cool and shaded
red brown cushion underfoot.

Rain will bring fantastic fungi
coral, brain and dead-man's-foot.
Blue and purple iris, sorrel,
shy calypso orchid spring.
Green translucence cool and shaded
red brown cushion underfoot.

Blue and purple iris, sorrel,
shy calypso orchid spring.
Saprophyte transparent white
hid from undiscerning eyes.
Green translucence cool and shaded
red brown cushion underfoot.

Saprophyte transparent white
hid from undiscerning eyes.
Tread a world of modest beauty
in this brief and rounded walk.
Green translucence cool and shaded
red brown cushion underfoot.

Susan Wolbarst

Proximity

Recently, I got really close to a dead pelican –
close enough to see the ring of pale pink and yellow feathers around
         its eye.
I couldn't determine its cause of death. No obvious injury. Lying there,
as if merely stunned, it seemed ready to stretch out its wings any
         second
and hop off the cliff, to glide over fishing grounds, or swoop down
to sit, kinglike, among the smaller seagulls on the sand.

I've been close to dozens of jellyfish, mounded on the sand
like jellied desserts encased in cookie crumbs.
Once I saw nearly a thousand shipwrecked chitons, their bright orange
         meat
partly ripped from jointed white shells by sea birds.

Pebbles, kelp, and driftwood decorate this cemetery,
alive with clouds of tiny flies and the background percussion of waves.
One is close enough to feel eternity here.
Footprints mark the way.

Riantee Rand

The Frogs

When the crispness of midnight
calls my body to water
I step naked outside my room
into a silence
like a damp shroud
slapping my body
short of breath.

The moon falls out of tune
and I know something is
missing
but I don't know what
it is
until dreams track
the absence
of what used to lull my flesh
into nebulous expansion:
                the frogs are no longer singing.

                Have we sprayed the deadly spit,
                cut short trees' trajectory once too many,
                have we imported the cannibal toads,
                have we made the language sin?

All night the moon calls the answer
hidden within the question.

Don't worry, keep moving
advises the dawn,
you have become corrupt staying in one place,
keep walking and you'll be whole,
walk woman's grateful curves,
walk that generous nipple,
walk slowly into surrender,
consider
how light falls equally on everything
foretelling a color for each creation,

walk and listen,
gaze through divine eyes
       hear the celestial song. . .

the frogs have always been there.

Kristine Hahn

Pond

This is where you forget to worry,
where you swim the first few strokes
and worries disperse in the wake;
becoming as invisible as the pond.

You don't call yourself a swimmer
but most days there you are swimming
always alone as if your life depended on it.
And it does.

The frigid water smacks
of the present – which is the point.
Here you are,
You are here.

Some mornings the bear has been there,
or still is. The murky bottom stirred
to the surface. No matter, you wait
your turn.

But more. There is a dependency
on religion of the morning;
better than other addictions –
you can think of many.

Little sips, you can't help
taking in little sips of sweet green water.
The ceremonial rinse upon exit
– seven splashes to the face.

Dog there. You whistle for him,
he perimeters the pond and wood
beyond. You think of your mark
on the pond: invisible but a mark
all the same.

Who doesn't love pollywogs?

That moment when you first saw a puddle a writhe
With tail and head and breathed the word, pollywog.
Probably non-PC now, tadpole, intones the biology teacher.
But really, consider the words, each derivation:
>   the tadde of toad with the pol of head,
>   but when is a frog a toad or vice versa?
>   Better the pol, head, conjoined with wyglen, wiggle,
>   so much more evocative of the state of being.
Wig to Wag to wog and in sailor cant, pollywog,
the newbie who has not yet crossed the equator.
But it's all a matter of position and time, that poly Cronus
moment of divide, the polymorphism of the body,
all the stages of evolution, that, we are told,
we shifted through, while in the puddle of our mothers' wombs.
Or polygamous, those wiggles of ovum penetrated
that tail of sperm, then extrusions of legs emerging,
one by one, that spread of web toes gripping reality,
From water to grit, land to green leaf
geometries of polygons amid the webs .
So evanescent, the time of change,
and everything keeps changing,
until all we can do
is call in the night,
knee deep   knee deep
Better go back   back,
knee deep
To that moment when we first saw
A puddle, a writhe.

II

A girl, her body just thinking about being a woman,
is bored, until she sees the puddles still wet
amongst all the other dips and hollows of earth,
cracked in the sun, marked with but tiny commas
where the potential of frog lapsed back into mud again.
She raids the car for jars, for milk cartons, and scoops up

muddy water squirm life.
Then hunts the adults, capturing four,
who pulse against the cage of her palms.
She will bring them home. It is science.

But what if they are bullfrogs? Those nasty eat every-things,
introduced to the watersheds of the north coast
on Frog Pond Road, at the turn of the last century,
Cultivated for restaurants in San Francisco.
But a rapid google search matches
the red-striped adults to Rana draytoni,
The California red-legged frog, endangered.
But even more exciting, brought to you by Mark Twain,
the Notorious Jumping Frog of Calaveras County.
No spoilers here,
just a tale of greed and chance and cheating.

But done with references, historical or otherwise.
She takes all home. While she might earn merit
raising the pollywogs to full frog-hood in her terrarium,
to release them into various shady spots for long lives,
she manifests a certain turpitude when she leaves the four adults,
contained, to sit in the sun.
They come to sere ends.

.

We can only hope they have each fulfilled their biological imperatives.

III

At the river she wades through shade and shallows,
armed now with pails and nets. She whoops with glee
at the size of the pollywog. Surely a bull frog.
When she dumps three clacking crawdads into
the same container the problem of the invasive species is rapidly
diminished. But then, inside the deep bucket, she reveals
the giant bullfrog, his eyes nictating, the membranes sliding,
as he looks into a grim future.
He cannot be released into her creek at home,
but she assures all involved in the deed of transport,
that she will deal with it.
A sharp knife, a pot of water, an internet recipe for dip.
To dine on crawdads and frog legs.

There are no Aesop morals here,
no charming Frog and Toad.

Just the eat and be eaten of life in a puddle of earth.

water song

tonight the water is singing
shhhhhhhhhh, lop, drop, plunk, shhhhhhhhhh, lop, drop, plunk,
shhhhhhhhhh, dink, clink, splunk, drip, shhhhhhhhhh
crooning a rain song in wind sloped pitch
falling, falling, falling into me
yet it is I, I who tumbles from limitless black
the vat of me wet like the ground

shhhhhhhhhh, lop, drop, plunk, shhhhhhhhhh, lop, drop, plunk,
shhhhhhhhhh, dink, clink, splunk, drip, shhhhhhhhhh

I want the sky to cling to my body
before it slides down and is swallowed by earth
I want the sky to rub its sheets of sound into me
to howl for me, chant with me
drown me in a poem so vast I am forever changed
I want the sky to drench my thirst
I want
I want
I want

shhhhhhhhhh, lop, drop, plunk, shhhhhhhhhh, lop, drop, plunk,
shhhhhhhhhh, dink, clink, splunk, drip, shhhhhhhhhh

I slip off my clothes and step away from these words
the night is liquid and I have escaped
for a little while
left the stove, its flaming madrone
traveled into an unknown midnight of march
flesh touching downpour
so water can
shhhhhhhhhh, lop, drop, plunk, shhhhhhhhhh,
its music
so water can
shhhhhhhhhh, lop, drop, plunk, shhhhhhhhhh,
so water can shhhhhhhhhhhhhhh
its music into the pores of me

I shiver as a gust rips at my edges
turns torrent sideways so it hits
like arrows from the dark
piercing me as I snake along this deluge
between time and transcendence
with the elements of rhythm
far too devoted to let death bewitch me
much too alive to witness war charm others
a chill draws me closer to the surface
of involuntary choices
I resist then yield

shhhhhhhhhh, lop, drop, plunk, shhhhhhhhhh, lop, drop, plunk,
shhhhhhhhhh, dink, clink, splunk, drip, shhhhhhhhhh

I am crazy, crazy with thoughts of those who come before and after
people who speak in seasons, gather seaweed, pack fruit up narrow
          paths
people before and after logos
people before and after our communities become consuming
          commodities
when we are oceans of bones cresting like redwoods
ancient forests flowing into each other
hearts knotted together
beating out the patterns of stars

shhhhhhhhhh, lop, drop, plunk, shhhhhhhhhh, lop, drop, plunk,
shhhhhhhhhh, dink, clink, splunk, drip, shhhhhhhhhh

I lay down
dumfounded and naked
in the soft, sopping duff
laughing with the gales threatening to tear off my roof
listening to oaks give up in thuds against the acres
how easy it is
to be alive
to grow old and die
simple as the planet cradling my spine

tomorrow I will walk the devastation
gather mushrooms rising in its wake

43

but tonight, I dance this water song
shhhhhhhhhh, lop, drop, plunk, shhhhhhhhhh, lop, drop, plunk,
        shhhhhhhhhh,
shhhhhhhhhh, lop, drop, plunk, shhhhhhhhhh, lop, drop, plunk,
        shhhhhhhhhh,
yes, tonight, I rain

Amy Scharmann

No Unfamiliar Place

There is a vast expanse of prairie
That tries to blow you into
The suspended sunlight
Leftover from dawn–sinking, subtle
(Light in all its forms can be confusing)

There are jagged bluffs
That should be unfamiliar
But the restless coastline of Mendocino
Is not so different from Kansas
And its tangle of grass
Bending with the threat
Of impossible yet unwavering hope

And here I am
Still riding the relentless wind
Of my own mind
Where I am and have always been
But didn't even know it.

Jeanette Stickel

Beach Grass

Long wide blades
of beach grass
bend gracefully in a breeze—
blades lift and lilt
with each breath of wind—
a troupe of dancers
warming up
for performance.

When the wind stops,
blades become
bodies bowed in prayer,
or aged ones,
hunched, rounded,
lift and lilt gone.

But at the bowed back
of every blade—
a silver sheen
of reflected light.

Each blade
a lithe dancer,
a quiet contemplative,
an aged one,
reflecting light.
All part of the dance.

Jane Galer

An Anticipation of Gulls

On the lip of the ocean
a thousand gulls sit the prayer of anticipation,
their soft hearts count the waves.
What oracle tells them of the storm none of us can see?
What instinct turns their eyes, beaks, and bodies north,
bracing, a collective decision, a momentary calling to order
interrupting the scrawl and cry and flightful chaos of bird life.
An anticipation of gulls, we slow to watch, the curving inlet
at the little river a towering but momentary shelter.
Later, the ocean will throw her will at them,
scatter them with the thud of logs
and crashing waves laden with sand and stone.
But now they are a warning,
unanimous in their attention, all arguing at bay.
And we watch the sky grow dark with wonder,
simple primitive selves,
hoping for a gale.

Land

Katherine Hastings

LORCA (Because Ghosts Can Go Anywhere)

> I'm coming back
> for my wings.
>
> O let me come back!
>
> — "The Return," Federico García Lorca

for Devreaux Baker

This morning I heard a woman has named
her puppy after me. Lorca! she sings.
Is his heart my heart? His nose my nose?
Together we celebrate our senses along the cliffs
of Mendocino. Our eyes are deep pools reflecting
our affection for the foam-blown sea. We roll
and rejoice in wildflowers and pine. I am love-struck
by this pacific world that carries no politics
on a rifle-bearing back so heavy with death.
Let us race down the path together, perrito,
grab youth by our teeth and shake it to the shore
where gulls rise on the updraft. The woman cries
Lorca! Lorca! but pay no attention, little one —
I have come back for my wings!

Note: "Perrito" is Spanish for puppy

Elizabeth Kirkpatrick-Vrenios

Psalms of the Headlands

Rocks hiss
pimple the shore
complain
as each white wave withdraws
drift of poetic clamor   ooh
ooh
ooh

Worn ruts
on sandy paths
dusty ghosts whisper here
invisible footprints
lead
me

Red/purple sheen
heaven's paintbrush
anoints ice plant's
color-blind clash
gut
tug

Golden poppies
open heavy skirts
lascivious bumblebees loop
shamelessly
drink
deep

Legs dusty
with pollen,
one lonely bee
coiled in a single red flower

naps
golden

Street smart
ravens hip hop
dagger dive somersaults
ride ecstatic skies
funky
whoop

Sun sets
I'm wide alive
each moment remembered red
through tarnished gunmetal skies
soon
dark

Foggy moonrise
dusts the horizon in abstract paint
cracks open the silver snakeskin
into dark blue
separates soul
from
body

Stars sing
the river's song
in deep flow down
in widening rings
that's why you must
walk so lightly
&
yet

Karin Uphoff

Uncovered

In her restless shifting, earth
reveals tresses of cliffs combed by
wind and rain and sun-bake,
a piece of northcoast, once under
forms a path trod over by many.

Here, you can amble like a rolling stone
in life's upwelling
where gulls break open perse mussels
to eat off rainbow plates
warm sun winks at shatterings of our past
ancient middens squint
in sky's bright scrutiny.

Come sit along the ripe edge of water
to mourn losses or confess crimes
let this rugged roiling add your story
to exposed pages of bistre, ecru, taupe
strata of shedding stars
layered volumes written in
surf's steady hand

incessant gouging holds
no escape except honesty
for the up-turned stone
uncovered
thoughts must reconcile
with the grand existence of things,
its waves of giving and taking away

Passing clouds may notice
but not judge, your
shameless capsized vulnerability
rocky shores of resistance
no match for these coves of death and renewal
squalls winnow away at pretense
to lay bare your amaranthine heart

as what you let go --- and what you don't
tumbles back into the surf.

Haley Hutchinson

To the kitchen, for filling

Torn basil
      and cubed crisp melon
I place upon a wooden cutting board.
Their separate piles complimentary
      in their greenness –
one's algal luster
the other, the sliver of sun
teasing a clear ocean horizon
the millimetric second
      the flash –
to see it twice would be lucky,
      not impossible.

In the morning, cages of
spider web crochet hang
strung among aster, yarrow –
      in the entropy
I seek pattern, a grid
that could place me
      a coordinate
on its axis.

Three canvas totes hang
on the pantry door handle, each
      softer with every use.
Grocery lists forgotten
      or completed
accumulate in their bellies.

These days I prefer to eat
      with chopsticks
slow and savored spice –
the last bead of brown rice
waits at the bottom of the bowl
      patient.

November is well-plated

like a persimmon sliced
into topaz eclipses –
plush and crunch, a single bite
        the orange flesh
lingering with the afterthought
        of winter.

Musing on the Still Life that is my Living Room

The round, blue skein of yarn
On the end of the bookshelf
Has a long tail which drops to the floor
And goes off, exploring.
It has a more adventuresome life
Than the ball itself—
Snaking over and between paperback books
Along the floor and up to a shiny bright-red bow
That had been tossed aside as a gift was unwrapped.
The soft blue tail touches this bow cautiously, a tentative attempt
To say hello and make friends, unsure
What reaction the glamourous bow will have.
The yarn is of some gossamer softness; it is
A fetching periwinkle blue, and thin
As a stirring stick from Schat's Bakery down the street.

Lean in, and here's a surprise: Close up
One strand becomes three, a trinity of soft colors,
One chromatically almost the same as the next,
Wound together like sisters
Into a single silky strand.

At another time, the ball of yarn might be picked up
And worked with crochet hook or knitting needles,
Becoming perhaps a scarf, or maybe socks.
The yarn within these projects might think itself more important
And mock the string on the books on the dusty floor.

I am ready to step up and champion the string,
Dispelling the partisan notion, stating
That this string, while just made of possibilities,
Is equal in worth for its beauty to my eyes,
And the creative muse it unwinds from my soul
Much as a tiny katydid clinging to a rose petal
In the garden beyond the window,
For no particular reason, might do.

Holly Tannen

The House That Once Was Mine

I burned all my journals on a January day.
Took my textbooks to the dump, and gave my birds away
To move into a handmade house one day in pouring rain.
I lit the fire and prayed I'd never have to move again.

The owners both were kind to me, a doctor and his wife.
They told me I could stay there in that handmade house for life,
Unless their son grew homesick for the ocean and the land,
And left New York to move back in the house they built by hand.

Roses fill the garden and tulips line the drive.
Their young son and his husband keep my maple trees alive,
But they've cut down the willow, the redwood and the pine,
And sun shines through the windows of the house that once was
            mine.

Now I live in a broken house beneath an orange sky
I pick the trash up in the yard and watch the well run dry,
While they sit in their garden, eating crab and drinking wine,
And show their handsome friends around the house that once was
            mine.

Jacquelyn Cisper

Cypress, Laundry and a Dog

deep green cypress,
purple velvet hill,
furry scent of dryer lint
from nearby hotel laundry,
soft drizzle drifts
across a brown field,
yellow dog, tight tail curl,
wanders, purposeful,
nose to earth,
to grass,
to seaweed smell,
late afternoon decay
of light and sight
of deep green cypress,
purple velvet hill.

Debra Ricketts

Diner

She served us greasy eggs
Thin ham and pale coffee
A well chewed pencil stuck
In her high gray hair

Donna Suzanne Kerr

Secret Doctrine of the Public Library
(Some thoughts on 24 years as a Mendocino County Librarian)

I wanted to guide
Eager young minds to knowledge –
I'm on my hands and knees
Cleaning a helpless adult's
Accident off the rung.
I wanted to be
A Bearer of Light –
I'm putting on plastic gloves,
And washing a homeless man's
Diarrhea off the bench.
I wanted to be
Wisdom's High Priestess –
But I'm on the floor
With our nameless resident
Who speaks to no one,
Who has just fainted
Three times from hunger,
Begging him to let
The paramedics
Bring him to the hospital.
I plead and call him by name
That secret I know –
A different sort
Of secret doctrine,
Of inner sanctum
Than I had expected
To preside over,
But perhaps, no less sublime.

And I have had my moments –
I have looked hard in the face
Of a hard young girl
Smiled, watched her soften,
And shyly smile back.
I have helped an old woman
Copy sheet music

Danube Waves
Red Roses for a Blue Lady
And seen her transformed
To youth by pure joy –
And I have taken aside
A rough old farmer
Read him Wordsworth's *Daffodils*
And looked up in time,
To see him cry for beauty.

Rhianna Gallagher

Eviction Notice

During a break in the storm

We are sitting on the stoop that faces west
Faces the only window of my bedroom
Looking at a stand of trees
Behind the house I rent from her
How they dance with chaotic grace
In the intense wind
She says her head hurts and she can't talk
But she sits with me for a while looking at the trees
What doesn't break you makes you stronger she says
I don't mean to be fatalistic she says
But I think the time for humans in this earth may be
Coming to a close
And after a short time, she moves to cut the hydrangea
Hydrangea reminds me of my Grandma I say
Yes they're old fashioned
I can't sit still for long she says
We talk about the rose for a moment
How she's holding up in the storm
I learned a lot from you about pruning roses I say
Yes she says you have to cut them down pretty far or they get too
                leggy
And she talks to me as she cuts the hydrangea
About how you have to take the old growth off for the new to come
And the black sage needs to be cut all the way down
There is a sweetness in her words
I'll take it as some kind of forgiveness
Maybe I am like one of these plants who requires to be

cut

Virginia Sharkey

The Moments When You Hold My Hand

The moments when you hold my hand

those crazy daffodils
pop up magazine-yellow

in the unkempt field at the corner
by the Albion store.

Not in March, not in April but far too early
too January-keen.

Though oh,
why not why not

all flittery
canary canary canary
through the greeny homeless grass.

Robyn Koski

Composting

In the season of curled, dried leaves and faded flowers,
weeds, decay and rot,
dead bracts shuddered against the wind.
They clattered a dry tune,
one octave below the chirping crickets
and one above the stuttering ravens.

The woman toiled with a shovel,
piling leaves,
hay,
sawdust,
horse manure
and rotting fruit in layers
that waited for the first rains
and the earth worms
who would hungrily finish the task,
turning their tasty home into humus.

As she dug the earth,
her shoulders and back felt the weight of each heft.
Her knees were fragile knobs,
bone on bone the doctor declared,
riddled with arthritis.
They creaked their frail song
to the vein that festooned her left thigh,
a curled, grey ribbon,
varicose.
When it appeared last year,
quiet and painless,
assertive in its relentless presence,
the woman greeted her new flaw with a shrug,
named it Wanda,
then washed, folded and gave away her shorts.

The hot sun sent trickles of sweat down her spine,
soaking the waistband of her jeans.
Waves of wind,
in low swells, minutes apart,

broke across her body
and she tingled with her aliveness.
The ravens cackled above, playing with the current,
glittering black and blue,
hovering strong in the fall light.
The woman felt weak and pinned to the earth,
between the worms and the ravens.

Every few minutes, she set down her shovel
and strode over to a rustic chair
where a spiral bound notebook waited
with a pen laid across it.
The woman sat
and gazed at the ravens with unfocused eyes,
fixated on something emerging from another realm,
to be funneled through her hand,
and her pen, then spilled onto the paper.

Her mind burrowed deeper than the shoveling task
and more elusive.
Its own layers were building
with characters piling on one another,
seething with desires,
emotion,
and conflict,
in voices distinct,
inhabiting a world deep and rich as humus.
Back and forth from the compost pile to the chair,
the woman paced from mindless task to mindful one
where she crackled with sporadic gusts of insight.

The woman looked up at the ravens
and yelled to them, waving her pen.
"The wind of conception!"
"I am your goddess."
"Bow to me."
"I created a whole world today where none existed this morning."
Then she stood,
stalked over,
picked up her shovel and raised it to the sky.
"Two,
if you care to ask the worms."

Marylyn Motherbear Scott

The Fuchsia

Vivid fuchsia, rich magenta,
larger-than-life blossoms,
all aquiver. Beyond beauty.
So alive I sense them singing,
I see them shimmering.
This moment wants no thing
but to gaze into presence, an adoration,
to bow and bend, sway and dance.

The rhythmic sound of digging
went suddenly, from in back,
turning the corner of the house,
to the side wall where, years before,
the fuchsia had staked its claim.
The terrain edged the porch,
gently and clearly held the space,
the place the plant and I shared.

The chinking sound of shovel
striking dirt brought me to my feet.
I rushed to where the fuchsia
spread her gangle of branches,
reaching to touch nothing
but air and light. The blooms swayed
in a gentle breeze, hung seductively
down from slim, fragile limbs.

The shovel lifted and fell. Words failed.
I saw the shovel's blade bite into
an exposed and now bleeding elder root.
In alarm, I screamed, Stop! The worker,
confused, questioned the matter.
Was the ditch not beautiful? It's evenly
sloped sides a perfect V. The shovel blade
rested in a deep gouge, a main root.

The old wood was sliced open, it's life juices

68

seeping out, wetting the blade. Soon enough,
the root could be removed to make the drain?
I shook my head no, showed him the trunk,
the limbs of this gentle plant, the bevy of
innocent blossoms that offered themselves
in profusion. His eyes saw, his lids dropped.
He was Greek and he understood beauty.

The boss wanted a ditch. He dug.
I rubbed dirt onto the wounded root,
protecting it from the sun while he worked,
continuing his task, now making his way around.
No matter. The damage was done.
Over the months to come,
the leaves withered and wrinkled.
Rust and black puckered their surface.

A cure by poison recommended;
I preferred to pick off each diseased leaf,
burning them to prevent the spread of illness.
Limbs became brittle, some broke.
Nearby, jasmine burgeoned,
entangling itself. A strangle hold.
Diminished in size, in stature, in bloom,
scabby limbs, a phantom fuchsia loomed.

Years later, cautiously, one venerable branch awaits
A springtime blooming. In devotion, I keep the watch.
Dead branches removed, excess pruned,
the surrounding plant-life cut back
creates a halo'd space around the fuchsia.
At its base, a small group of hopeful stems
reach for the light. My breath reaches, too.
We whisper to each other, in fuchsia and magenta.

Nan Trichler

Storms Pass

The night train of weather
rolled in on schedule
greeting our sleeping town
Traveling across the Pacific
In the black hours
gathering up oceans
and air currents
delivering them in torrents
on our used up
mill town off the coast
of the ocean of oceans
What builds up
way out there?
In darkness
What forces and why?

I so excited
waking to a charcoal sky.
Remember yellow skies
in the south growing up
remembering red tides
and hurricanes bending
palms to the ground
hurling coconuts
like cannonballs
at boarded windows.

As children we nestled
in the security of
our parents' assurance
that storms pass.
My brother and I
awaiting the wonder
of the Eye
teasing our fate
by racing to the beach
to witness the indifferent

damage of waves
swollen with tropical revenge
against the obstacle of land
and the man made
assault of his intentions.

There was never enough
time for our eyes
to experience the
full magnitude
as the storm circled
back on itself
and we hightailed
home to our sanctuary
behind storm shutters.

There is still in sleep
the narrow roads
water on both sides
the family car driving onward
with water all around us.
The road disappears
and the car takes to the water
gliding like a duck
noticing the change
but unafraid
the dream retells itself
through the REM "time
of my life"
and I rest endlessly
in the security
that storms pass.

Tonijean Bernbaum

We Are The Wine

One of the best reasons to steal away
is to share this perfectly aged wine,
and fall in love
all over again.

Twelve years into the meat of you
and still some distance from the bone,
I'm undaunted by anything you might
employ to resist me.
none of that matters
in the curve of a moonlit spine,
none of that can keep you from the answers
I was born to give.

We know we have everything to lose
so we keep getting better at letting go.
We're old enough
and wise enough
to love like there's no tomorrow –
rip the halter off the last mare
let the wagon wheels fly back to the barn.

We are like this wine
seeds of desire bursting with sun,
the sweat of the growing season,
the crush between our toes,
we are the calloused hands,
the flowering vines entwined.

We are the time
it takes to age.
We are the harvest.
We are the drunk,
the king and queen
toasting to love eternal.
We are the last drop –

The empty oak barrel.

Cathleen Micheaels

Waiting For What Will Happen Next
for Jennifer Plattner Wilkinson

To be that much part of the world again,
to be caring and loving not to everything but

to just a few small things—like our neighbor's
granddaughter, who as a young girl loved all

birds wild and tame, gentling stroking the feathers
of her grandmother's silky laying hens the way

some young girls would the mane of a favorite horse,
carrying wild bluebirds home in the inside pocket

of her coat, the steady rise and fall of her breath
calming them and later when she was older,

spending early evenings luring a particular
young kestrel into her hand-crafted snare, then

taking the bird with her everywhere, even to dinner
at her grandparents' house. Once while I was visiting

that not yet tamed hawk perched suddenly on top
of my head and I held very still, not frightened really

but carefully taking in and letting out each breath—
waiting for what would happen next.

Melissa Eleftherion

Page of Wands & Magnesium

At last
it got dark enough

to stand on the blue stoop
each of us, one hand on hip,

the other hand holding a coarse wand
aloft our gazes lit by the cherry

stub of my father's cigarette
his hands now rainbows

now pinwheels
now catasterism

of motion & light
as we wave our bright sticks

of magnesium & sulfur in the air
spell our names with bubble letters

& perchlorates
Wield our swords of lightning

& force
Holding grownups at a safe distance

as they detonate M80s in the street
a rubble of exhaust & debris

that will continue to emit
for days after, a thin veil of smoke

as we run, chased by errant "jumping jacks"
the blare of baseball radio

from every backyard on the block

we waving, magic & dirt thick in the air

& under our chins
there on the blue stoop

two new star systems becoming visible

Caryl Thornton Sherpa

The Magical Qualities of Thyme

Time,
Language is funny like that.
One measures seasons.
The other is measured to season.

One heals.
The other counts our days.

One, we nurture to harvest,
The other limits our yield.

What if we wore a thyme piece around our wrist,
Each embrace, fragrant with possibility?

What if we planted and tilled time,
Gathered and wove it into garlands, then danced?

A cure for melancholy, antibacterial, antiviral,
One lengthens life.

An ill for eras, our error, each hour
Calls death closer.

Evolve to know,
Nature is infinite as are our days, so

Sing of *Thymus vulgaris*
And our many, many, many long lives!

Katy Pye

Wolf Signs
(On fearing my daughter may have lupus)

I found scat on my boundary today
At the edge of the worn turkey path
Where hens with chicks lively troll
For seeds and small juicy bugs,
Alive in the short browning grass.

I found scat on my boundary today.
An early test marker dropped
At the edge of the narrow tree line.
Crouched on lean, muscled haunches,
Lupus' shadow waits silently panting.

I found scat on my boundary today.
Fat edges plumped tightly with hair.
Cells dry, stiffened, and turned.
A being's bits now marrowless bone.
Death rests in the browning grass.

I found scat on my boundary today
At the edge where fear scrapes its toe
Against our ancient DNA line.
A troubled breeze circles fence posts
And futures hang pinioned on wire.

Kate Dougherty

El Niño

Five days before your first birthday
we old ones shake our heads –
Has it been a year?

Your father smiles at us
that being his answer
He has come for manure
for his garden, he comes to visit
and likewise give your mother rest

But it is labor to heave that stuff
so wet with the weight
of a winter's rainfall
and to carry you too
on his back…

Come here little one
the sun is warm
the muck is deep
and I have not held a child
for much too long

You struggle
and fuss but we stay near to him
as he bends to continue
his cadenced work. In time
you relax into a trust
that melts your body
into mine
and close to my heart

Pointing your finger you begin
Dat?   Dat is horse
Dat?   Dat is another horse
Dat is Slip horse
Dat is Haddie horse
Occasionally you'd turn

and ask pointing your finger
Buzzard
Sky
Redwood

How many times you asked
for Dat I did not count
but after a while
I try to wrap it up
with the sweep of an arm –
Dat is universe

Marina laughs and says
it will be really funny
if he ends up thinking
the forest is the universe

True.   A mystery
I slipped in between
pointing to your bellybutton
and the sun

Silent Paintings

First Painting

Background:
          A sweeping brush stroke of pale grey
          watery, streaked
Middle ground:
          Dappled light
          wide expanse of orange and burnt umber
          golden mustard yellow
          brown vines gnarled and twined
          around each other
          touching Earth
Foreground:
          Naked poplars
           tall and elegant
           their thin branches undressed
by wind and time
          as they continue to reach
          inward and skyward
           at once

Second Painting

Background:
          Dark grey steel blue
          thick clouds
          Low ceiling
          of dramatic sky
           dancing
          Feeling the rain
          wanting to burst
          to drench the land
           become One
           with

Middle ground:
          Pale green-grey clear salty waters

Faint glimmers
　of Light and Hope
on the horizon
always the hypnotic motion
of undulating sea
Silent
　from a distance
Always the song
　heard clearly
if one is immersed
in her vast music

Foreground:
　　Wheat-colored fields
　　　invisible wind
　　Grasses waving
　　　slowly greening
　　leading
　　　to sharp edged cliffs
　　where only seabirds dare
　　　to dance
　　or the occasional errant deer
　　　or fox or human
　　explores the boundary
　　　between known
　　　and unknown
　　or the night owl
　　　dressed in downy brown
　　　and white speckled feathers
　　　brushes the air
　　　in his silent hunt
　　　　claws and beak prepared
　　　　to dive
　　　　to devour
　　　　　prey

The silence of Earth
is not quiet
It is a loud prayer
beckoning us to listen

Listen,

then

Return

Home

Susan Lundgren

Mendocino Neighbors

A lone quail perched daily on the rustic wooden fence,
tall black topknot, round grey upper chest, alert and proud.
From her window, the woman with long gray hair watched in quiet.
New to town, and knowing no one, she looked forward to his
        presence.

One day, while clearing empty breakfast bowls,
she noticed movement in the grass below—
mama quail at the helm, three striped, fuzzy babies,
father scampering closely behind.

The woman remembered a time long ago when her own child
played in their flower-filled suburban backyard,
long before the daughter moved thousands of miles away,
to a life of her own.

Days later, cries of distress pierced the neighborhood,
plaintive, persistent, painful to the ear.
The quail couple perched on a nearby fence,
calling and calling to unseen children.

The woman's heart stopped, remembering stories
of birdlings carried off by red-tailed hawks,
like the one she'd seen atop the nearby ancient water tower,
head turning slightly, eyes watching, ready to pounce.

The next day both parents reappeared, three babies in tow.
Relief in her soul, the woman recalled when her own child
wandered and could not be seen, her panic, her fear,
and then joy when the girl stepped out from hiding.

She watched all summer as the three little quail
grew into adulthood, knowing they too,
as time passed, would move on
to create their own lives.

Anna Levy

The Gifts

During the pandemic, I –
it's hard to explain, but –
perhaps you had to be there.
My brother in Brooklyn could
only walk around his block and
only at certain times; his world
became the street where he lived,
where neighbors banged pots
and pans every evening, to thank
health care workers returning home.
We did that here too, timely
solidarity across a continent, and
together apart with my neighbors, I whooped
from the front porch, where I stood with
my furry, black dogs, who had become
my constant companions.
My world got bigger then, strange to say but
true because of the child
– so wanted, so unexpected –
growing inside me and because here,
in this rural nowhere, I had room to roam.
Every day, I walked by the ocean,
the one I'd claimed as my own,
remembering there were people on an unseen,
opposite shore, banging their pots,
banging their pans. I walked by nasturtium and
calla lilies growing like weeds, calla lilies that have
long reminded me of a wedding in
Montana years ago, where the bride
carried them in her arms like jewels. I
walked through wind and rain and fog,
for no illness can stop the weather,
and stayed inside when raging fires
burned the silent world in their reflection.
Because nowhere is exactly here, friends
left gifts on my porch as my child grew:
kale from a backyard garden, a homemade bumper

for the crib that someone else handed down
to me. Here in this nowhere, it is the gifts
that are made with brilliant hands,
that are grown in gardens, that
have already had a home, that are the
most precious. My friends brought
warm bread wrapped in dishtowels,
and drove me to appointments, masked,
where I went in alone to watch my child
dance. Under the generosity
of this community, my little one grew.
And when the day came, we left this town,
for babies do not arrive on the coast.
Stopping halfway to stand under a confetti of
snowflakes, I gazed toward the gray and rare
and reverent sky.
We were told not to leave our homes.
Yet there, before the hours of labor,
before the hours of pushing, before
that new California landed in my arms, I
held the future to my mouth,
and kissed it.

Asmar
"Thus saith Muhammad ibn Ishaq [al-Nadim]:
'The first people to collect stories, devoting books to them
and safeguarding them in libraries, some of them being written
as though animals were speaking, were the early Persians.'"
And this: "Ibn al-Nadim refers to fictions as 'evening stories' (asmar),
as one was not supposed to spend the daylight hours
on such idle stuff."

— Night & Horses & the Desert: The Anthology of Classical Arabic
Literature, Robert Irwin, Editor,
The Overlook Press, 2000

I am here to tell you such a story. It is night, we are here, in Ukiah. It
is a time of dreams and fictions. There is much to say, about the town
and its planet, about our fragile hold on its crust, about the vast world
of stars. And I speak to you under the cover of darkness because that
has always been a time when things can be said that could not
otherwise be unsaid.

Eleven centuries have passed since al-Nadim first wrote about
devoting books to collecting stories. A car bomb explodes on
Mutanabbi Street in Baghdad. It is the spring of 2007. Mutanabbi
Street is the historic center of Baghdad's bookselling, with bookstores
and outdoor book stalls, cafes, stationery shops, tea, and tobacco
shops. Pretty much just like School Street here in Ukiah.

It is a mixed Shia-Sunni area, named after the tenth century Iraqi poet,
Al-Mutanabbi. More than thirty people are killed and more than a
hundred wounded. And the books burn. The area is destroyed. It
takes a year and a half for the street to be reopened.

"The Suq al-Warraqin, or bookdealers' market, in tenth century
Baghdad, contained one hundred booksellers." It's exactly like School
Street. "Some of these shops doubled as literary salons and, for
example, Ibn al-Samh's bookstore provided a rendezvous for
philosophers. Medieval bookdealers often branched out into the
manufacture of paper and the copying of manuscripts."

So these stories that we tell each other, this culture of majlis—of soirees—at which poets and scholars strut and compete and tease each other with their wits and send words on wings to devour our souls… you must now imagine that it contains a silence inside of it that goes on for a year and a half. A century and a half. A millennium and its half. That's nearly 60 million heartbeats for each one of us. Imagine the musical composition that could encompass such a silence.

Which is why I am here to tell you a story. It is night, a time of dreams and fictions. There is much to say, about School Street and its planet, about our fragile foothold on this crust of earth, about the vast world of stars. We are in a garden. Your lover is nearby. She is wearing a cloak of dark purple; he is perched on a stone wall covered with lichen and he plays his guitar.

Speak softly, then, or you will disturb the heart of the night.
Speak quietly from the balcony that overlooks the garden.
Toss me your scarf because the moon is wounded.

Walk softly on the balcony overlooking the gardens.
Toss me your scarf because there has been an explosion and I am dead.

The garden is gathering the dew in its throat.
Speak tenderly on this balcony overlooking the flowers and the vegetables.
Toss me your scarf I am losing my soul.

Kelly Barrett

Mendocino Graduation

A teenage boy
riding a bicycle
tows a boom box speaker
blasting the song
Should I go or Should I stay now?

Another boy,
on the edge of becoming a man,
drives at a high pitched speed,
gunning the accelerator, vroom,
through the streets straight out of town.

Flowers are blooming everywhere.

Monique Sonoquie

Alcatraz

3am   drowsy   foggy   blurry   cold
silhouettes   feathers   hats   gloves   blankets
Sage   Sweetgrass   Coffee   Copal
Rising upwards towards the Creator

Prayers for a Good Day
Thinking about the first ones on canoe

The next ones jumping in
The weight of
wet shoes   jeans   salt
red blooded determination

The far reach to the shore
Hard rock under hand
Pulling them up to her
Embracing them   Loving them   Thanking them

Today
Thirty-five years   Big boat   Warm faces   Greetings
Drums   Clappers   Heartbeats   Vibrations of ancient
First timers   One timers   Every yearers
Organizers   Activists   Singers   Dancers   Spectators
Elders   Babies   Wanna bees   Instigators   and
Bad Ass Indians!

For many a dream come true
Bucket-list   a Journey   a New Beginning
Together walking to the stars
Following smoke to the fire
Singing and dancing with Our Ancestors
Ceremony with Grandfather Sun
Few have seen your beauty like the Indian has…

This is Indian Land

Jan Corbett

The Land Taught Me

"Run through the fields,
but beware the unseen holes,
brambles and rocky paths,"
the land whispered

As my horse and I soared over fields of childhood,
Heads up, ears forward, listening, and learning land.
I learned strength, fearlessness.

I saw that land as smooth curves and rises, much like a human torso,
Lithe, but powerful.
Also vulnerable to change, shifts, but always offering dialogue.

Land invited me to play, work, create hidden retreats from the world.
And though, through time, the structures I built crumbled, and land
                    was sold,
Land remained patiently understanding.

That land shaped my dreams, hopes and yet speaks to me as I walk
past those fields.

I yet feel the late summer sun and grasses over my head as I lie
in my own bed of memory.

No wonder men and women have died rather than give up their Land.
It is sacred. It becomes part of us.

Leslie Wahlquist

Poetry in Motion
Wyoming

My broad-backed mare stands apart from the herd, a quiet zone,
a nuzzle, dusty brush, strip of leather slipped around her muzzle.

The forest is sharp with ragged limbs, gray and spare, last night's
frost hangs in the air, clings to the north of the trough.

Gentle my reins along the narrow deer trails, leaning close to her
neck up the hills and away again down the steep rocky dales.

Near the edge of a meadow she prances, ears taut to an urgent
breeze whispering through long, dry grasses. Come dance it pleads.

A circling hawk cries and she snorts a reply, head tucked, stamping
and pawing at dry earth she awaits my signal to fly.

We pound out three beats, now pounding four, atop thunder
I rest, the drum of her hooves sounds deep inside my chest.

Momentum fills my ears, my nose with wind and eyes with tears.
Under a keen autumn sky we are the beat of poetry, this mare and I.

Barbara Mackay

Journey to the San Rafael of My Youth

San Rafael once had an aboveground unnamed creek
Which ran parallel to 1st street
Where my grandmother lived and where
My sister and I spent our summers

We spent our afternoons gathering wild berries
Exploring the overgrowth of trees, bushes, brambles on the far bank
The evenings exchanging stories of why fireflies lit up the twilight
Or how a croaking frog turned into a prince charming, or playing Go
       Fish

But it was the mornings I loved
Tadpoles circling, water spiders dancing and the current
Rippling toward the culvert where it disappeared
And ran underground to where I do not know

The early sun gave enough light for me to see a few feet into the
       culvert
Then all was dark and the white paper boats I fashioned
Sailed into the unknown and I would have followed them
But for fear of never surfacing and knowing my mother would miss
       me

Today walking along the sidewalk
That now covers the creek I put my ear to the ground
I hear its song as clear as the birds chirping above me
I shed my shoes slip into the culvert
And let the downstream current carry me
To my childhood of long ago

Valley River

See it running through fields of alfalfa and interloping wild oats, chasing after the sound of tight gut strummed over exotic woods crafted by the ones who know the music that must be played for the heart disappearing into green turning to sun beaten gold, valley floor the sacred anvil of the hammering sun, birds in flight with the ghosts of childhood memories: legs browned by summer, sweet fruit dripping juice licked up by thirsty tongues. Down among the boulders of the river we found a snake going about the business of slithering into and out of the edges of the stream. We let it go its way, seeing no need of capture for a classroom of squealing youngsters.

We found the devils darning needles recounted in bedtime stories by the grandest people of all – our parents and theirs, dreaming out loud what they heard by firesides and woodstoves, places where proper meals were made, sparks flying up from logs burned to embers, banked against the night fled into by souls in search of everything lost, found in a single visit to the valley hidden away amongst the shoulders of hills begging to be climbed; behind them their cousins, the mountains, blue with rock and ice and white with snows that nourish all the creeks and streams that flow to make the one river we all come back to after all, racing through the valley, searching, finding what was once lost in the blink of ages.

Charlotte Gullick

Google Maps Can't Take You There

There's no re-creating the memory. Not enough unraveling of the highway through a screen. No approximating the way a vine-plucked blackberry flames in the mouth with late July heat.

Google, with its capturing eye, cannot travel around the corner and up the quarter mile dirt road. It cannot pass the barn, where hay and horse and saddles and reins haze the air.

Technology, friend and foe, cannot approach the sound of dad's chainsaw or mom's canning tomatoes or one sister tangling with Chopin at the piano nor the other sister's prayered susurrations or the snap of the cotton sheets, laundry on the line.

Or the gasp of the school bus brakes, reliable Howard opening the door and his face to us.

Or the hole in the bathroom floor we all pretended wasn't there.

The water stain on the ceiling that grew each sun-scarce winter.

The way my father cupped his hand around my mother's waist. Once every in a while. My father's brown skin against my mom's pale, pale, pale.

No camera holds the image of mom and us running, running, running in the dark from dad; only our own minds know the waiting on a neighbor's front door after Mom's knock. Our own hearts thrashing from the dash, from the fear.

Nearby, redwoods, poised and prudent, stand in their abiding height.

There's no street view to allow you to enter our afternoons informed by a cow's blue low separated from its calf for branding.

Or the sudden whoosh of an oak succumbing to snow and gravity.

Or cat tail puffs punctuating the autumn afternoon.

Or the rumble of the garbage truck—dad coming home with the dignity he claimed.

The rain falling and falling, fog informing the valley. Dad up at 3 am to check the road, to ensure the channels he'd created held the churning back, our access to the outside world narrowed down to his physical attention.

The tang of beer salting a shirt and the air, a rattle of a snake's tail feet away from your bare leg.

Google cannot admit itself to this place so off the map, this place both golden and
haunted, this spot of no easy access.

This that is mine.

Nancy Horrocks

Before Leaving Home

I needed to step outside and hold my world together.
Well, at least I needed to think that I could do it.
There beneath the great trees who hold up the sky.
I needed to try.

I needed to watch the newborn fawn with legs all wobbly,
to look deep into her eyes still innocent with wonder,
then see her turn and nurse so simply on her mother.
I needed to believe.

I needed to see three tiny red heads poke hesitantly
out of an old hole in the tan oak as they did every year,
and hear concerned acorn woodpeckers whistling round me.
I needed their embrace.

I needed to lift my face up to the winter rain
and feel it soothe my skin and mingle with my tears
to hear the wind run wild through oak and fir.
I needed that reassurance.

I needed to be rocked to sleep in the movement of stars,
and awakened in the night by comforting conversations of screech
                    owls
in the light of a waning moon.
I needed a lullaby.
I needed to go out in early morning, as vultures filled the snag
spreading their black wings wide to dry against a yellow sky,
so I could be where life and loss are understood as one.
I needed to cry.

And I still need to be where all around me is as it has always been,
where hills and valleys, mists and fog, light and dark,
and trees and birds and all that lives, lives in me.
I need to go out…and hold my world together.

Patty Joslyn

Spirit of Place

Home is a place in the body.
It sits against the walls of the heart.
Bangs around in the darkness,
breathing its way into moments.

I am lost, she whispers to the night sky.
It winks at her.
I am a fool, she tells the same sky.
It does nothing but listen.

She wonders if home might be a place she's been,
and has yet to visit the Finger Lakes or Morocco.

She's been known to call the past home
the future, too, though she lives in both.
Being here now means so many things,
but not the address on the front gate.

She lives as if neither weather nor traffic matter.
Black ice and earthquakes equal nothingness.

She has books high on tables.
She wants angels in the snow.
She wants a crown of daisies,
and to give away all the gold.

She wants to feel at home.
She wants the same for you.

Marlis Manley Broadhead

Meditation on Mary, Full of Grace

Eight seasons since we danced above Mendocino,
music and laughter lacing the trees turning charcoal
in the summer night. In Chicago, seasons are less
kind. Skyscrapers slice the icy wind into shards, and
summer is a sauna of concrete and steel right up to
the lake. I ride the Metra east to resurface at Union
Station and am swept with the crowds across the river
that ripples with water taxis and tour boats, past the
panhandlers' cups rattling in the long shadow of Willis
(Once Sears) Tower, and I try to imagine you folding
into a lotus flower on your smooth mat in the silence
of your upper room where you've told me you empty
your mind, a skill learned in India when your young
head was full, yet open. Tell me, how does one learn
to not think of all there is that makes up a life?
How to slip into some quiet gray crevice, ride a single
breath into a cavern of tranquility, and not sink into
the void of fathers, retrace the wayward path of
a distorted inheritance, stumble over a mother's footfalls
that circled from a distance the lodestones of losses.
And are there never technicolor flashes of the affair
that brought the great gift of Grace, your new beginning
swaddled and perfect beside you in the cabin in the
woods? This strangely mild summer day tantalizes me
with everything I miss along the coast where your love
and laughter are a refuge. I do not expect to discover
a path to tranquility. Awake, my mind is a kaleidoscope
of all that was and couldn't be and may or may not yet
come true while I search through the tumbling
possibilities for patterns by which to shape a life.
Asleep, I dream of Mendocino, the imagined landscape
of a life that could have been, only to awaken in
the middle of the country wondering what
you're not thinking about now.

Cat Spydell

Grays

Silver mists rise over the Anderson valley,
doom weather of rain and darkness

yet

as I drift through country roads
on my way to the Ukiah hospital
where my daughter is
giving birth to my first grandchild

the roads are gray and wet
the clouds gray and thick
the rain on the windshield,
gray reflections of a gray sky.

I arrive on time and the baby is born.

Later on the drive home
to Philo on the ridge,
the sky and roads
and rising mists
are still gray

but this time I notice

the deep green of tree moss
along scraggly scrub oak branches,
and the dark purple hues that abound
in fields of lupine
blooming alongside the road
on every turn,
violet bright smiles
in the monochrome haze.

It is as if the earth
is shouting

"Welcome Baby Grayson!"

Jan Allegretti

I Saw the Face of God

I saw the face of god today. Greens and browns and blues, mostly. Light filtering through, creating all manner of shades and hues, patches of yellow and darker greens. Brown limbs arching, moss caressing the graceful lines. Each grand tree reaching to another and to me...alive and soft, moving and gentle in the breeze. And waterbugs dancing on the surface of the creek, zipping back and forth, hopping now and then, chasing breakfast. A buzzard sailing across the patch of blue between the treetops, wings spread motionless, head turning from side to side surveying her creation. Not a feather moves as she soars for miles.

I heard the voice of god today. The creek gurgling over a rock behind my shoulder. Crickets chirping, locusts humming. The leaves whispering in the breeze. And a lizard running through the grass, sounding like a small dinosaur.

I felt the touch of god today. The softest breath across my cheek. The air a perfect mix of warm spring sun and cool shaded breeze. The rocks beneath my seat and the cool creek to wash my face. The grasses brushing my legs and the bite of a mosquito. The love of the trees as they hover around me, loving me and the others, the community of radiance of all life of all forms of all energies and beings. The breath within my lungs fresh and sweet and clear. The joy in my heart and the knowing that I am the rocktreescreekbugswindlizardsairsunskyearth.

I learned a song of god today. Singing the bliss in my soul for all the trees to hear. A song of thanks and awe and happiness.

Naty Osa

A Pelican Flotilla

Perhaps today I'll mobilize
a Pelican Flotilla, unauthorized couriers,
pouches stuffed to bursting, and, unabashed,
we'll shower fishes on a troubled land.

Perhaps stunned soldiers will look up,
spear fishes with their bayonets, roast them
on the raging fires, put their wrath down
with their guns, and invite all to partake.

Perhaps we'll all get on our knees,
pray that our respective Lords will turn
the bombs to loaves of bread, bile to wine,
and rain compassion on a love-parched land.

Perhaps children will come out to play again,
clear a field from the rubble, pick a team,
run to score, not out of fear. And, when the ball falls
over the neighboring fence, it will always be returned.

Erica Lutz

A Change Has Come into My Color
(after Vincent Van Gogh)

A change has come into my color since you were here.
First, I turned green at the gills, then the green of new life,
Spring's newness pushing against the dead grey of old rose stems.

Yes, then pink! those months of flowering cherry blossoms! Small
        roses!
My watering eyes due to allergies, I tell myself.

I have been for years the color of a sturdy yellow field,
resembling the self myself was when you left.

Star thistle and beggar tick, dusty clay, vole holes, ants and paper
        wasps.
I've had my last flush of heavy fruit weighing down boughs.

A change has come into my color since you were here.
"If you ever sell this house," my old father says, whose color
fluctuates gray to pink, "make sure you sell it As Is."

In this same kitchen fifty years ago, my sister and I compared the
colors of our mood rings. Purples and greens.

Grief

Grief is never too far away. Clings
like kelp to a dead seal. Like ashes
to your shoes. A million orange sunflowers
exploding in the sky. Never too far away,
the deer running towards your car
eyes pressed against the windshield.
Red mud cracking beneath your feet. The
anemone in the desert.

Clean up day at Van Damme State Park. Seven
pounds of trash. Fifty-four cigarette butts.
Thirty-four food wrappers and the business
card of a noted local naturalist. He met
his wife at a garbage dump, both chasing
a rare gull. Died recently of unnatural
causes. Grief never too far away.

It finds you when you least expect. Falling
light of late afternoon filling the music
room, dust settling gently upon the cello
and piano. Your hand resting like a boat
in a harbor. Upon my back.

Grief is never too far away. The bark
of the world stripped one tree at a time.

Liz Helenchild

For Naomi/ Ear to Earth

Rain at last.
Ear to earth for chant of
Chanterelles
Hydnum repandum
Hydnum umbilicatum
I am
Hunting & gathering forest coin
Tossed like spare change of golden doubloons
Spendthrift spindrift of fungal bounty.

Bellying under huckleberry & manzanita
On forest duff amidst a maze of understory
In search of hedgehog mushrooms in scattered clusters
Each sun-colored cap almost incandescent
With tiny teeth beneath

I think of you, Naomi,
Felled by shattering loss
Your only son found dead of Covid.

Feeling you maybe
Stretched out low & listening
On unyielding Texas caliche
Surrendered beneath merciless sky
Seeking a pulse a heartbeat a glint
some underground conduit
To your sole son
I send you love love love
All the way down the mycorrhizal line.

I would comfort you, Naomi, at my kitchen table
With a platter of succulent sautéed morsels
On a hank of steaming linguine
At the forested edge
Of the world.

Annie Brenner

Fall

Yesterday our garden was full,
Of all the girls we nurtured and
   helped grow
They were our companions
   from Spring until Fall
They listened to music, drank
   tea and grew tall
They reached for the sun
   and sometimes the full moon
And we gazed in amazement
   as their crystal flowers bloomed
They listened to us
We listened to them
And next Spring
We will grow them all over
   again
But this morning a warm tear
   falls from my eye
As I wish them good luck
And tell them good-bye

Robin Rule

Prologue to This River, This Road

This road I walked first time the autumn of 1975 now the first part of
        '94
Cold hard wet winter la niña all mud potholes   land slides
& huge old broken trees to walk over or around every winter another
        one
This road carved out by settlers in 1868
but before that walked by Huchnom & Pomo
who hunted here ahead of gingham and glass beads
& before that a deer train
& still a deer trail for buck   doe   bobcat   bear   quail
& small children hippiefied & wild in early spring mornings
going to two-room schoolhouse after all this rain

This road follows the creek which turns into a river which turns far
        north into the sea
This road once the stagecoach route Black Bart & all
& men gambling on land & giddy women in eastern finery eating the
        West
as dust pours into the wagon like creek water every summer of no rain
This same road once Mexico became U.S. in 1848
tried to secede to Ecotopia in the 1980's & before that
tried all the smoked-up mojo tricks & tripped out backtotheland
        tragedies
of the late sixties & early seventies

The road is the river
The river tells everyone's secrets & old stories in a language
we understand between sleeping & waking
Dizzy underneath willows & bay laurels in the afternoon sun
half-listening to God's country radio where water
splits the atoms of past present & tomorrow

The creek is the river   is the neighbor who gossips between dreams
talks turkey over the back fence in summer   yaks up a storm in winter
delivers us the good news & squawks out the calamities of end days
In spring when we drop seed into gigantic holes hidden in the woods
our fingers crossed   our prayers leaping into the air like grasshoppers

106

We hear the floating voice on the water
There is no shutting her up

Michelle Blackwell

Yellow Dust

Yellow dust swirls in the current
alighting on every surface
I breathe in the powder of life's origin
a poor vassal for its value

I've seen photos of the particles
hitched to legs of buzzing beings
Today, the specks are visible
ubiquitous, pervasive, everywhere

She rolls on the sun-warmed concrete
her black coat turns green
The absence of color
mixed with hues of yellow

Does the bee know it creates life?
Does the cat know she makes me sneeze?
Hachoo
Hachoo
Hachoo

Gwendolyn Dakin Johnson

Spring

Winter slowly thaws, as spring softly approaches.
Clouds part, revealing sweet daphne and narcissus.
Sun warms the hardened earth
coaxing purple crocuses to push through the soil.

Brook tumbling down the mountainside,
sun's warmth melting the ice.
On the banks reeds poke green stalks through
the marshy soil.

Quince orchard nestled between green hills,
trees old with twisted, tangled branches tied with vines.
Brambles fill the spaces between
as buds begin to form.

Earlene Gleisner

Complaint of a Redwood Tree

I was meant to rise into the sky,
To capture the fog and the wind, embrace them.
Bring the waters into my core,
Stand firm against the gusts to protect
Life on the land.
I was meant to be with others of my kind,
To communicate and nurture
Through our shared roots.
I was meant to live into centuries,
Not crashed to the ground, sawed apart,
Nailed back together into another form,
As a deck or shingles or a shed.
I was meant to preserve The Earth at my feet,
Keep the terrain intact.
I was not meant to be taken for another purpose,
Leaving the soil naked
To wash away in every rainfall,
Tumble into once pristine waters.
I was meant to be here forever,
Not just as a memory in picture books,
Read by children who face their days
Trying to survive
In a wasteland.

Marty Durlin

I Wanted to Learn From the Trees

But they stood silent
They presided but they
didn't speak
I walked among them
daily, almost daily
waiting for their wisdom
They loomed, some leaned
They took the space
They swayed, offered shelter
but they did not speak to me

They were teaching by example

Dot Brovarney

The Engravers*

Males sensing weakness
bore through
scaly silver-umber skin.

Within the flesh
they prepare the nuptial chamber
secreting pheromones — their siren call
for female companionship.

Expectant mothers
construct egg galleries
birthing young by the thousands.

Parents and children
mine plant sugar
thriving on vascular tissue

Their bodies the tool,
engraving.

what remains:
a trail map,
a work of art,
mortal wounds.

*the engraver beetle (Ips.spp), the size of a grain of rice, attacks
stressed pine trees, including the bishop pine on the marine terraces
of the Mendocino coast. Sources of stress include drought, disease,
overcrowding due to fire suppression, and the presence of logging
slash.

Danielle Mucho

Twilight Embers

The day dwindles to a fine line in the fire,
smoking the air with its last embers
as it flickers into night's darkness;
all aubergine and neutral colors alike drained by the evening's breath
and wisped away,
leaving behind only still silence in the wake of night.
And to fill the void,
the distant lights illuminate one by one,
sprinkling their nutmeg light across the valleys
and upon the barely flickering embers of the fire pit,
still glowing spice orange amidst the charred wooden logs.

Kirsten Ellen Johnsen

Today, the Grass is Running

Today, the grass is running.
In one morning, it has grown long enough
to bend in waves racing up the hills.
Why is this pleasing?
Somehow it tickles my heart
to see the wind so manifest
and the rounded slopes playful.

There is more to be offered, they say.
For one moment on the wheel only
before the baking heat crisps the land to gold.
We are supple, we are alive.

I remember one year the rain stayed so long
the grass kept growing into June, still green
so that when the wind blew the skirts of the land
they undulated.

Each separate stem bent, bowed, rebounded, and then bent once
        more.
In unison, they flickered so
that my eyes danced dizzy upon the vision
of the whole world rippling.
At any moment its veil ready to part
to the pure power behind everything.

Now I know it's there, always,
waiting.

Air

Here

Winds rake across the headlands and disrupt the skies,
sucking breath from our noses and mouths.
Vultures, gulls, ravens hang in the sky, riding the thermals,
slowly cycling, beaks cocked, until wide wings suddenly tip.
In the upwelling of air where sea and cliff face meet,
healthcare and housing, crises of immigration, racism, politics, prisons
plundering communities, ravaging our lives.
White caps rise and stagger across the impassive plane of the sea.
I lean out in freefall, then pump my strange new wings.

Karen K. Lewis

Wind Whistle
(for every lost child)

Whistle bird, whistle. Hiding behind dawn mist.
Whistle, child, whistle. Hiding in tree fort.
Whisper, wind, whisper. Dancing with ten thousand trees.
Tree holds a fort. Fort holds a child. Child holds a dream.
Bird swoops from sky.
Whistle bird, whistle.
Child stretches arms. Imagines flight.
Whistle child, whistle.
Bird lands on tree.
Silent child. Silent bird.
Eye-to-eye. Courage flows.
Child. Bird. Tree. Sky.
Touched with dawn light.
Cradled by moon memory.
Bird holds child. They fly free.
Fly beyond war. Beyond smoke. Beyond pain.
Child becomes bird. Whistling to dawn.
Bird becomes cloud.
Carried by wind.

Laura Pope

Naked

I just now see how brave I am
coming from that thorny nest
where my voice did not count
where I was invisible
and had to be
Chancing on a path
that led onto a stage
I walked out on a careening high wire
over crowds
doing a dance I never rehearsed
speaking a poem out loud
in the instant I was writing it
Not feeling up to the mark
I dropped my robe
on the stage
in the spotlight
and I realize
just now
this is the merit
My gift is not the work
it is the showing up
in the face of fear
and loneliness,
and not being enough
Speaking truth
though my voice shakes
and my knees tremble
This is the gift I give
the gift you have to offer
our nakedness
our bravery
The real work is stepping up
stepping out
in the glare of the spotlight
dropping the robe

Alonya E. Lowe

Return

I had forgotten
the thick wetness of the air.

My nose drips,
a crumpled tissue balled in my pocket,
a relic of pockets past.
This dampness,
the culprit of cunning mold problems
and nightly sneeze attacks,
the reason Pop moved three miles inland
to escape the ever-encroaching fog bank.

My yearning to return
had become too loud and so,

bundled in puffers
we brave the enveloping blanket of drip.
"This was my childhood!!"
I practically shake my husband by the collar,
as if this cold misty air
will somehow make him
understand me more deeply.

A raven perches upon the eerie angel statue
at the top of the bank.
My husband snaps a pic with his cell.
I do not bother with my fancy camera.
I am fourteen again,
and I am annoyed
by the unrelenting grey void
where the sky should be.

I silently urge my hometown
to come to life
so that my spouse can see:
in the sun,
the ocean sparkles

and invites toes to dip in tides;
in the sun,
the Victorian homes
are no longer haunted;
in the sun,
I fall madly for this place again.

I know I cannot will the fog away.

Closed in by nauseating winding roads
and encapsulated by nippy mist,
bursting young me was
so restless here.

And now,
propelled by a profound longing to return
I find myself captured in the damp
once more.

I expand my adult lungs,
breathing in the wet fresh air
of the town that raised me.
My body loosens
as I come to the same conclusion
of some twenty years before,
a conclusion
that makes me want to weep
into the fog:

I simply cannot stay here.

Mendocino,
I love you with all my heart.
I have to leave,
but I'll miss you like hell
like I always do.

Lynn Kiesewetter

Seagull — Ode to Gordon Black.

You and I met some 50 years ago, Gordon, working at the old Seagull
          Inn-
     "Fine Food and Lodging"
       and an arrow pointing down: "The Cellar Bar,"
       said the signs.
We all got to be friends,
after work engaging in banter,
     philosophic discourse,
     musical analysis,
     grammatical fine points,
     comedic one-upmanship,
and yes, I dare say, yes, sigh,
       flirtation, and other nonsense.

Ahhh, the old Seagull.... quite the roost ...
a non-stop parade of notables, characters, outlaws, flaneurs...
And the crew, equally colorful, hand-picked by ringmaster David
          Jones,
     among them you, Mitchell Zucker, Bill Bradd, Tony Miksak...
It was an honor to be there in that midst....
     an honor and a challenge; you boys kept me on my toes!

And now?
     Gone, the Seagull, the Cellar, the jovial camaraderie,
     gone, too, all you boys........
Our friendships lasted the decades, didn't they?
Sometimes riveted, energetic, argumentative, hilarious,
     and other times,
          radio silence,
          ships passing in the night.

But it was always you,
Gordon,
you
     who pushed me, pulled and prodded,
     lured me further:

122

You can!
You could!
You ought to!
You need to!
  Write it! you said.
  Read it! you said.
  Sing it! you said.
  Play it! you said.

Without you, would I have?
  Could I have?
  (How would I ever know?)

Thank you, dear heart,
you were the wind beneath my wings.

Now it's your turn to fly.

Katherine Fengler

Whiteout

Whiteout, reduced visibility
watch for indications of hazards
stay still, breathe, assess.
then keep on moving
keep on.

I am in the snow, further on.
come find me.
call my name.

It's so cold, the past echoing
through the deep hollows
below the drifts
words lost in the wind
no language.
repeat
after me
I
I am.

Come find me.

If you walk backwards
count backwards.

count backwards by sevens.
do it again. Start from 100.
I'll be there, in another language
on the very edge of the seven's cross
holding on.
waiting.

In some past life
I lifted you out of the water
were you breathing?
I lifted you out, that's all I know
and you will love me forever

for that
for this

Take my hand. In the bright sun-
light we can dance
on the ice of the frozen mind
sing songs of springtime, pull
the living from under the snow
speak in tongues.
Ninety-three. That's it—
keep on going. eighty-six, seventy-nine.
surprise them all.
"Backwards, backwards
lift the curse
backwards, backwards
Disperse!"
Find me.

Rebecca Patyten

Suicide Survivor

I've let go of my dark past and the trauma that ensued.
It doesn't matter now, and it never will again.
I'm true to myself and all those around me.
Standing strong with ambition, I'm proud of who I am now.
Looking back, I remember the agony of those days.
I moved with pure intentions and kissed the pain away.
I'm on my way now to where I'm meant to be.
I'm tucked into a reality where I'm happy and I'm free.
I've dreamt of these days, of these internal rays of sunshine.
Wanting the best for society and the Earth—humans and animals
        alike.
I fell in love with smiling and wanting to hold your hand.
I'm in a different dimension now, and it's stunning where I stand.
I see you and me together, and I hope someday it's true.
The world is so different now than it was before.
I let go of all that was weighing me down,
So I can now dance freely and soar.
There's this one simple thing that's never really changed.
It's deep within the core of me and the center of all things.
It's my heart that's made of gold, and surely it is known.
With two gems in my eyes that sparkle as I gaze,
I'm so happy I survived suicide to live my life this way.

Alyson Sagala

Somewhere

I wonder what it would be like
to live in the velvet underbelly
of my forgetting,
in the place where every favorite sweater
I ever lost disappeared to
in the place where I won't grow old,
but can finally grow up.
I want to live in a place
where my skin is always perfect
and every door I want to walk through
is unlocked
a place that's between dreaming
and being awake
where all the extras in the background
have the faces of childhood
friends I no longer talk to.
I am always surprised
by the number of people I know
who are dead.
Remembering they are gone
is like learning how to swim,
that dropped stomach feeling of
realizing the bottom
is out of reach.
I want to live in a place
where fruits left on the kitchen counter
never rot,
where maggots don't exist
to chew the muscle off
softening bone,
where people I miss
and won't ever see again,
are simply hiding behind hallway corners
like children playing hide and seek
waiting to pop up,
and scare me.

Kit Bliss Jones

Shades Of Remembering

Just when you think you know
That's when the wind will blow
To a time that is pure spirit
And in your heart you knew it

It was so perfect in time
All essence did rhyme
You were so very tall
Truth was known to all

A yearning drove you to come
To earth and become one
A calling pulled you here
For goodness to be near

A welling felt in the throat
An aura covered your coat
Love stirred from within
With a chance to begin

All things were known
All clarity was shown
A big chance and opportunity
To make your mark in eternity

How brave you are
This work will take you far
My throat swells with love
Feeling the soft touch of a dove

Do decide to step up to the plate
Open to you who has this fate
It is for you, the one who is great
Time is now and it is not too late

Amanda Cruise

i navigate human spaces like i'm swimming underwater

tell me you do too
tell me you hold
your breath at times, wonder when
or whether you can surface to grasp
cold air into thin lungs

tell me you want to swim to solid underground
become old growth forest far from
wherever here is from
whatever this is

wake up instead as
madrone skin in bright sun
usnea hair after rain, mist
rising, scorpion grass blue yellow
iris eyes invasive with spring

lose the need to talk out loud altogether
move into sandy earth and redwood duff
ospreys nesting and tidal riverbeds
becoming

people a dull roar receding
this is home, this is my home
the light electric
this place of being
certain i can finally resolve

into wherever here is
into whatever this is

tell me you feel it too

Joan Stanford

Moon Musing

You asked what the moon is to me
I said fullness, completion.
Did not mention light in the darkness
Which it is, of course.
Or muse for sonatas, poems, nursery rhymes
(lovers gazing at, cows jumping over)
Or puller of tides, disturber of equilibriums,
Cause for howling.
Did not mention that it teaches of cycles
Of faith, of return
Inspires dreams, explorations
That the moon pulls us to look up, beyond
To gaze into the wonder of it all
The vastness of it all.
No matter where we stand our eyes see that same moon
No matter what we are going through
What heaviness our hearts carry
That milky, round eye
Witnesses with compassion.

Priscilla Comen

Place Of Spirit

I don't want to let him go
And yet I know, I know
That place is calling him to come
As if he might be going home
I sit by his bed and watch his chest heave
It seems hard for him to breathe
My husband my love for seventy years
We had only smiles, no tears
He belongs here in this place
Yet I must let him go to that other place
Where I will meet him there one day
And we will renew our vow to say
I'll love you always.

1945

I dream of you
lines of you in
dirt and ditches
still
comprehensile or beyond, like

Broken bone
china oddly laid
on lonely tables miles
long abandoned,
no longer gathering memories.

Still you speak-
voices, echoes, sighs across
even the still air and
cruel vacuum of the open fields
and barbarous wired fences.

Our meager hands
our largest dreams
cannot hold
enough
of you.

I Say Choose a Stone

The wind's always pitching
for an argument—stirring things
up is what she's meant to do.

Clouds are content to roll
with the punches.
Rivers, endlessly restless,
are happy waving goodbye.

Birds can't help but flit and squawk.
And no one can distract a tree
from her earth-scented life of prayer.

But a washed-up stone wants nothing
more than to sit in the palm of your hand—
to go home in your pocket,
take up residence on the sill.

You can count on a stone to listen
to the grievances of your potted plants
and figurines. The door to her dark
little house is always open.

No story is too sad for a stone.
Every pebble has been to the bottom
but can often speak
of the view from the highest peak.

Tia Ballantine

Staying Aloft

Geese overhead today
not in V-formation
but they honk just as loud.
Flying north and east,
they stay apart, separated
by a pulse between, a space
stretched wide, growing
wider still, each bird
a wing-tied knot
attached to silken sky.
Flight laced to distance,
a shimmer net, cradling
the still beating world heart,
keeping it from sudden collapse.

Sally Carter

Fogging In

There is a heaviness in the air
The wind has finally stopped
Fog manifests this weight
Gently scurling into the treetops
Close to the coast
Softening the edges
Blurring the horizon with the sea
Today we do not look outward
We peer inwards into lit windows
Books, ovens, minds
Seeking identifiable form
Comfort from the oncoming
Storm.

Chrissy Sullivan

A Sound Quilt

Is the noise I hear
The wind high above
Passing through the
Fir branches and around?

Or is it from traffic
Along the highway inland
An eighth of a mile it's found.

I listen now to many birds singing
They seem to take turns
But also blend their sounds.
I'm more certain the source is
From perches above the ground.
Named species specific
Their songs fill the air and
Time with a sequence of notes.

Repetitive patterns
Together in concert
Give this place a distinctive
Quilt of sound.

About the Contributors

Zomala Abell has lived 56 years in Albion. and shares poetry in gratitude for family, friends, community and the vitality and beauty of our planetary home.

Jan Allegretti is a holistic healer and an advocate for nonhuman animals and the natural world. Her relationship with the wild lands is foundational to her life and work.

Devreaux Baker is Poet Laureate of Mendocino County, has published five books of poetry, won numerous awards, and curates the Mendocino Open Mic Poetry Series at the Mendocino Art Center.

Tia Ballantine lives for peace, paints, and writes in Fort Bragg. After publishing eight books of poems including *A Mineral Fact*, she's completing *NO WAR*, a hand-drawn anti-war book.

Kelly Barrett has been writing, gardening, and practicing yoga in Mendocino since 2013. She lives with her partner Michael among a marauding mob of raccoons, manic hummingbirds, and pollen-intoxicated bees.

Henri Bensussen (shc/hcr) lived for 17 years in Ft. Bragg, active in the writing communities and with the Mendocino Coast Writers' Conference. An essay on her garden is forthcoming from Wild Librarian Press.

Susan Schaefer Bernardo lives in Gualala. She is the author of five books for children including *Sun Kisses, Moon Hugs* and *The Rhino Who Swallowed a Storm*.
www. innerflowerchildbooks.com

Tonijean Bernbaum lives in Fort Bragg. When not writing poetry, she is facilitating healing groups at Spirit House, doing Tarot Readings, making collage art, and tending the garden.

Michelle Blackwell is a freelance journalist and writer living in Fort Bragg. Her fiction has appeared in Writers of the Mendocino Coast anthologies. "Yellow Dust" is her first published poem.

Annie Brenner is a bartender, farmer, mother and poet. She lives in Leggett and enjoys laughing at life and herself every day.

Marlis Manley Broadhead is a former college instructor, MFA Fellow, award-winning author of novels, short stories, and poems. She founded the Mendocino Coast Writers' Conference and now lives and writes on a horse ranch in Kansas.

Historian and author **Dot Brovarney** writes about humans and the natural world. Her recent book, *Mendocino Refuge*, explores life in a North Coast canyon. www.mendocinorefuge.com.

Sally Carter lives on the Mendocino coast where she also paints and gardens. Recent work appears in these anthologies: *Transitions* (Writers of the Mendocino Coast) and *Best of the Best 2024* (California Writers' Club).

Jacquelyn Cisper lives in Fort Bragg and works as a self-employed visual artist. She enjoys spending time in nature, gardening, and cooking. Find more of her art and writing: https://jacquelyncisper.substack.com/

Priscilla Comen sold stories to *Modern Romances Magazine* sixty years ago. Now she works at Mendocino Community Library and writes book reviews for the *Mendocino Beacon* and *Advocate News*. Six grandchildren and one great-grandchild inspire new writing projects.

Jan Corbett is a retired English teacher, living with her significant other. She loves participating in all the arts; most of all she loves spending time with her grandchildren and their parents.

Amanda Cruise lives in Mendocino on Northern Pomo land. Her poetry, printing, and art have appeared in publications and galleries in the US, Europe, and Asia.

Sharon Doubiago has authored many books of poetry, memoir, and essays. She began writing a month after moving to Mendocino in 1974, inspired by the place and its poets.

Kate Dougherty moved to the Mendocino Coast in 1978. She co-hosted Wild Sage Poetry with Dan Roberts on KZYX&Z for many years and loved teaching poetry to children of all ages.

Marty Durlin is a poet and musical playwright. She lived in Mendocino County for five years while serving as manager of KZYX, and now lives in rural Colorado, working as a freelance journalist.

Melissa Eleftherion is the author of many poetry collections including *gutter rainbows* (Querencia Press, 2024). Born & raised in Brooklyn, Melissa manages a branch library, curates the LOBA Reading Series, and is Ukiah's Poet Laureate Emerita.

Maureen Eppstein's most recent poetry collection is *Daughter* (Finishing Line Press, 2024). Her work has appeared in many journals and anthologies and has been nominated for a Pushcart Prize.

From **Karin Faulkner's** perch at 80, to the frightened child fiercely writing, life from then to now has been a multilingual, multinational festival of voice, paper, pens & poets ablaze in Words & Truth.

Katherine Fengler is a queer activist, poet/dreamer living in Fort Bragg with her partner and animal friends. She first came to Mendocino County by bicycle from Canada in 1972.

Jane Galer writes poetry reflecting her interest in the intersections of the natural and esoteric worlds. Her most recent book is *Forward & In the Dark*.

Rhianna Gallagher is a multimedia artist living in Eureka, California. She has exhibited in the USA and Europe. Her work can be seen online at rhiannazoegallagher.com

After 22 years living on the Mendocino Coast, **Harriet Gleeson** retired to the Bay Area with her partner and their dog in 2023. She has begun writing again after a taxing moving experience.

Earlene Gleisner lives in Willits. She has published essays, short stories, memoir, and poetry including *Reiki in Everyday Living*, *The Marriage Bundle*, and *The Sacred Bundle*.

Georgina Marie Guardado is the Poet Laureate Emerita of Lake County, California, a Poets Laureate Fellow with The Academy of American Poets, and President of the Mendocino Coast Writers' Conference.

Charlotte Gullick grew up in Mendocino County and is a novelist, essayist, and educator. Some of her nonfiction appears in *Brevity*, *The Best of Brevity*, *Pembroke*, *Dogwood*, and *The Rumpus*.

Kristine Hahn's first poem publication was in her university's literary journal in 1995. Her current poetry collection is called *Things That Do Not Touch the Earth*.

Gwen Hardage-Vergeer raised six kids in inland Mendocino County. She works as a speech therapist and loves to ponder about life while at home or in nature.

Katherine Hastings, Sonoma County Poet Laureate Emerita, has four full-length collections, most recently *A Different Beauty* (Spuyten Duyvil, 2022). She retired to an island in the Niagara River and returns to California annually.

C. Rowan Hawthorn is a poet and bookseller who writes mostly for herself. She has been published in small journals and the Writers of the Mendocino Coast Anthology.

Liz Helenchild is a wordslinger, radio DJ, dancer, Texpatriate, sometimes fashion illustrator, ESL teacher, taxista, crisis line counselor, and volunteer chaplain. Grateful Mendocino resident since 1972. Once locked eyes with the Dalai Lama.

Nancy Horrocks moved to Mendocino County in 1989. She has always loved writing and poetry. Her awe of nature, good friends, and family have inspired her writing and curiosity.

Haley Hutchinson is the Editor-in-Chief of Write Bloody Publishing and a bookseller in San Francisco. She is a graduate of Middlebury College and the Columbia Publishing Course.

Kirsten Ellen Johnsen lives on Greenfield Ranch. She is a weaver, mythologist, and ceremonialist providing spiritual care services for hospice and climate grief. She publishes poetry and essays. www.kirstenellenjohnsen.net.

Gwendolyn Dakin Johnson lives in Ukiah and likes to spend time in nature as well as reading books by authors such as Edith Wharton, Isabel Wilkerson, and Elif Batuman.

Kit Bliss Jones started a diary at 12 and has participated in Toastmasters and poetry groups in Palo Alto, Redwood City and Point Arena. Now 79, she dreams for all your wishes to come true.

Patty Joslyn lives on the Northern California coast. Her work has been published in *El Calendario de Todos Santos*, *Still Point Arts Quarterly* and in anthologies. Patty mourns the loss of doing cartwheels. www.22pearls.org

Mary Rose Kaczorowski is an artist, photographer, and journalist published in *The Berkeley Times*, *Vahalla 8*, and *Midwest Poetry Review*. She's featured on KZYX-Z radio's *Rhythm Running River* and at Cobalt Gallery.

Karen Kellam has shared poems in *Keeping Time* by the Monday Morning Poets of Sonoma County. She's a retired Santa Rosa Junior College counselor/instructor and participates in the Hardy Girls writing circle.

Retired librarian **Donna Suzanne Kerr** lives in Willits. She has contributed to a *Poets on 9/11* anthology, been a ukiahaiku Festival winner and keynote speaker, and authored two poetry chapbooks.

J. Redwing Keyssar, RN, is a poet, author, Palliative Care Nurse/Educator and Midwife to the Dying. She leads weekly Poetic Medicine sessions online. www.redwingkeyssar.com

Lynn Kiesewetter is a jazz pianist and singer who lives in Fort Bragg where she also composes and teaches piano. Current projects include a collection of short stories and a CD of her music.

Elizabeth Kirkpatrick-Vrenios' third book of poems is *Concerto for an Empty Frame (Kelsay Books, 2023)*. Nominated for four Pushcarts and Best of Net, she has published in numerous journals and anthologies. https://kirkpatrick-vreniospoet.com

Robyn Koski is a Writer of the Mendocino Coast. Her short stories and essays are featured in many of the WMC Anthologies.

Kristan M. Larsen, poet and songwriter, was raised on the Mendocino Coast with decade-stints in NYC and SF. She participates in open mics, writing workshops, and loves the local writer's community.

Anna Levy lives on the Mendocino Coast, where she works as a licensed counselor.

Karen K. Lewis lives between Salmon Creek and the Navarro River. A longtime California Poet in the Schools, her most recent book is *Peace Maps: Poetry*. www.wordjourneys.org

Alonya E. Lowe is a photographer, writer, and performer who grew up in Mendocino and currently lives in the Pacific Northwest. Find her work: www.alonyaphotography.com

Susan Lundgren retired in Mendocino after 30 years as a college counselor and psychology instructor. She volunteers in Fort Bragg as an English reading tutor for Spanish-speaking families. www.SusanLundgrenWriter.com.

Ericka Lutz lives in Fort Bragg. She's a well-published novelist, poet, and CNF writer who dabbles in clay sculpture, solo performance, and creative procrastination. Find her virtually at erickalutz.com.

Barbara Mackay is published in journals and anthologies including *American Tanka, Finishing Line Press, Writers of the Mendocino Coast*, and *Thema*. A native of San Francisco, she has lived on the Mendocino Coast for 20 years.

Janice Marcell was born in Fort Bragg, California and has resided in Mendocino County most of her long life. She has been writing poetry since she was a young girl and loves the spiritual connection writing and reading poetry often provides.

Ethel Mays, born and raised near the skirts of California's Sierra Nevada, has shared her art and writing with diverse parts of the world. Her soul has never left California.

Cathleen Micheaels carries out integrated literary and visual arts partnerships with K-12 schools, colleges and communities throughout Northern California. She lives in Elk but keeps a foot in San Francisco.

Point Arena Poet Laureate **blake more**'s work includes performance poetry, video, murals and teaching with California Poets in the Schools. blake hosts a monthly poetry & jazz series and two radio shows. Find out more at <u>bmoreyou.net</u>.

Danielle Mucho, a young poet currently attending Pacific Union College, aims to capture the little moments in life through her poems, and help inspire awe and curiosity of the world.

Nancy Wallace Nelson lives gratefully in the redwoods east of Mendocino. Nancy writes, reads, and walks as she breathes in the forest and ocean. Her ongoing memoir project is "Growing Up White in Racist US".

Linda Noel, Native Californian of the Koyungkowi tribe, grew up in Willits and is the former Poet Laureate of Ukiah. Her work has been published in numerous journals and anthologies.

Lauren Oertel is a writer and community organizer based in Austin, Texas. She writes poetry, novels, short fiction, and short nonfiction. She attends the Mendocino Coast Writers' Conference every year.

Naty Osa takes long walks along the Mendocino Coast and at Chico's Bidwell Park. Both abound in poetry.

Artist, writer, and coastal resident, **Rebecca Patyten's** poetry has appeared in *Word: Mendocino Poets in the Schools Countywide Poetry Anthology* (2008-2009).

Laura Pope is an accidental poet in Fort Bragg. She has worked as a painter, jeweler, mixed-media sculptor and is finishing a music CD with a music partner.

Katy Pye's debut novel, *Elizabeth's Landing,* earned four book awards in 2013. Her passion for pollinators created a gardener's workbook, *I Spy! Who's Using My Garden?*

Riantee Rand was born in Paris, France. After traveling the world, she and her husband settled in Mendocino's redwoods, where they built their house. Her poems and prose appear in magazines and anthologies all over the US. Her books and children's stories are also in print.

Lorna Humphrey Rauscher is the mother of two awesome grown children who were born and raised on the Mendocino Coast. She also has two wonderful grandchildren. Poetry is her creative outlet.

Felicia Rice, a Mendocino High grad, recently returned to town after a 50-year absence. She is a typographer, letterpress printer, internationally-collected book artist, and the founder of Moving Parts Press.

Mary Catherine Rice is a retired educator and arts education advocate, currently living in Fort Bragg and exploring the natural beauty of the North Coast in words and watercolor.

Debra Ricketts has enjoyed Maureen Eppstein's poetry classes and readings. She's participated in writing workshops with Suzanne Byerley, Charlotte Gullick, and Lisa Locascio. Debra works in Fort Bragg as a Registered Nurse.

Robin Rule has lived in Mendocino County since 1975. She moved into a 2-room cabin on 10 acres when she was 18. With woodstove & spring, she settled in to write.

Alyson Noele Sagala is a writer from San Jose, California, currently based in the Anderson Valley. Her writing is focused on the intersection of place, identity, and our relationship to land.

Amy Scharmann holds an MFA in fiction. Her work is widely published, including in *TriQuarterly* and *Joyland*. She writes, teaches, takes pictures, and lives with her partner and children on the Mendocino Coast.

Marylyn Motherbear Scott's poetry, prose, and theatre pieces are widely published and performed globally. Motherbear moved to La Honda in 1967, the Summer of Love, and now lives in Albion where she's writing a memoir.

Diane Semans lives in Surfwood with her husband Bill. Their daughter, Anne, directs the Kelley House Museum; daughter Sheila directs Noyo Center for Marine Science. Diane's memoir is *From the Shore to the Sea*.

Prartho Sereno's most recent collection is *Starfall in the Temple*. Poet Laureate Emerita of Marin County and a Poet in the Schools for 21 years, she teaches "The Poetic Pilgrimage" online: www.prarthosereno.com

Virginia Sharkey, an abstract painter creating tone poems on the deflections of time, is also a violinist in the Symphony of the Redwoods and the Mendocino Music Festival.

Caryl Thornton Sherpa lives and gardens in coastal Mendocino County, where the landscape inspires her lifestyle, community involvement, and writing.

Monique Sol Sonoquie, cultural practitioner, presenter, author, organizer, and activist, is passionate about youth empowerment, cultural education, and dedicated to empowering Indigenous youth to embrace their identity and traditions sonoquie.wixsite.com/sonoquie

Cat Spydell is the author of four published novels and lives off-grid in the redwoods near Philo. Her calico cat, Athena, accompanies her on many adventures. https://bookshop.org/p/books/epona-s-gift-cat-spydell/16509790

Joan Stanford, innkeeper, poet, and art therapist believes in the power of the creative process as reflected in her book, *The Art of Play: Ignite Your Imagination to Unlock Insight, Healing and Joy* (She Writes, 2016).

Jeanette Stickel's poems have appeared in *Spiritus, Sojourners, Fathom, Ekstasis, WayWords, The Orchards Poetry Journal, Canary* and in the anthology *Homage to Soren Kierkegaard* (Wiseblood Books, 2023).

Janferie Stone has lived for over five decades on the Mendocino coast. She explores the world as a mother, Aikido practitioner, teacher, gardener, folklorist, and peripatetic poet, occasionally published.

147

Sondra Sula is a writer and artist living in Fort Bragg. She has authored six books, most recently *Meditations on Mendocino*. Her work has also been published in anthologies.

Chrissy Sullivan lives in Mendocino. She edited and published a creative nonfiction local history book, *Wheeler: The Wolf Creek Era* by Georgia Sullivan (Third Beak Publishing, 2023).

Folklorist **Holly Tannen** sings traditional ballads and her original songs, including "Eat Your Triceratops", "Downstream from Dylan", and "Somebody's Wrong On the Net". http://hollytannen.com/home.php

Damieka Thomas is an MFA student at UC Davis. Her publications include *The Noyo Review*, *Glassworks Magazine*, Poets.org, and *Rejected Lit Magazine*. https://www.damiekathomas.com/

With gratitude, **Nan Trichler** devotes this life to family, quilt art, poetry, Buddhist practice, gardening, and nature. She has lived in Mendocino County (several locales, rural and urban) since 1970.

Joycelyn Trigg moved to Mendocino after a career in scholarly publishing in the South. She holds an MA and an MFA. Her new poetry collection is *Vital Records* (Finishing Line Press, 2025).

Karin C. Uphoff is an herbalist and author of *Botanical Body Care: Herbs and Natural Healing for your Whole Body*. She is working on her first poetry chapbook. www.karinuphoff.com.

Leslie Wahlquist lives in a renovated barn in rural Mendocino. Her stories and poems delve into the natural world and intimate relationships. Her writing appears online, in magazines, and anthologies.

Cate White, painter, writer, podcaster, performer, and roadside witch leads a cult for people who really just want to believe in themselves. Visit www.catewhite.com to learn more.

Theresa Whitehill's most recent book, a collaboration with book artist Felicia Rice, is *Heavy Lifting*, from Moving Parts Press. She is a former Poet Laureate of Ukiah. www.theresawhitehill.com

windflower recently moved to Western Massachusetts with her wife. Her poetry is internationally published in journals and anthologies. *Age Brings Them Home to Me* (Finishing Line Press, 2024) is her recent chapbook.

Susan Wolbarst lives in Gualala, where she presents a "Poetry for Everyone" event each April at Gualala Arts. Her new poetry book is *It's Over* (Finishing Line Press, 2025).

Clare Bercot Zwerling is a some-time poet and participates in the Fort Bragg Library Poetry Workshop. She also knits ravenously.

Credits / Permissions

Jan Allegretti, "I Saw the Faces of God" was previously published in *Listen to the Silence: Lessons from Trees and Other Masters* (Tenacity Press, 2007). Printed with permission of the author.

Tia Ballantine "Staying Aloft" was previously published in *A Mineral Fact* (Lelepono Press, 2024). Printed with permission of the author.

Jan Corbett, "The Land Taught Me" was previously published in *Balm of Yelapa* (Azalea Creek Publishing, 2021). Printed with permission of the author.

Maureen Eppstein, "What Matters" was first published in her collection *Rogue Wave at Glass Beach* (March Street Press, 2009). Printed with permission of the author.

Jane Galer, "An Anticipation of Gulls" was first published in *The Spirit Birds* (Poiesis Press, 2012) and also appeared in *Outskirts* (Poiesis Press, 2016). Printed with permission of the author.

Harriet Gleeson, "Charmed Circuit" was previously published in the anthology *Fire and Rain: Ecopoetry of California* (Scarlet Tanager Books, 2018). Printed with permission of the author.

Earlene Gleisner, "Complaint of a Redwood Tree" was used to support the protests of logging in Jackson Demonstration Forest, 2022. Printed with permission of the author.

Kristine Hahn, "Pond" has been published in *Things That Do Not Touch the Earth* (Poiesis Press, 2024). Printed with permission of the author.

Nancy Horrocks, "Before Leaving Home" appears in *Feeding the Hummingbirds: Poems & Writings* by Nancy Horrocks. Printed with permission of the author.

Karen Kellam, "Shoreline" previously appeared on poetrylovers@lists.sonic.net (May, 2024). Printed with permission of the author.

Kristan Larsen, "Scattered" has been performed with live music. Printed with permission of the author.

Ethel Mays, "Valley River" was published online by A Room of Her Own Foundation (AROHO) Printed with permission of the author.

Cathleen Michaeals, "Waiting for What Will Happen Next " was previously published in a slightly different version in the chapbook *The Idea of a Perfect Angel Cake* (Mt. Ararat Press, 2005). Printed with permission of the author.

blake more, "water song" was first published in Godmeat (Beatitude Press, 2008). Printed with permission of the author.

Danielle Mucho, "Twilight Embers" previously appeared in *Blacklight: The Invisible Inc. Anthology* (2024). Printed with permission of the author.

Laura Pope, "Naked" has been performed live on the radio. Printed with permission of the author.

Felicia Rice, "Lift" was previously published in *Heavy Lifting* (2022) and in *The Heavy Lifting Companion* (Moving Parts Press, 2023). Printed with permission of the author.

Diane Semans, "Come See Me" was previously published in her memoir *From the Shore to the Sea* (2018). Printed with permission of the author.

Holly Tannen, "The House That Once Was Mine" first appeared in the Writers of the Mendocino Coast anthology *Common Ground 2023*. Printed with permission of the author.

Karen C. Uphoff, "Uncovered" previously appeared in the Writers of the Mendocino Coast anthology *Erosion* (2021). Printed with permission of the author.

Theresa Whitehill, "Asmar," Copyright ©2009, Theresa Whitehill, All Rights Reserved. Commissioned for the event, "Vigil for Iraq: Original music and poetry honoring the dead, the wounded, the grieving, and the dispossessed" (Ukiah, CA: Ukiah Players Theatre, producers; Friday, October 16, 2009; performance videotaped); previously unpublished. Printed with permission of the author.

windflower, "Grief" was originally published in *Beyond Words Magazine*, November 2023. Printed with permission of the author.

Susan Wolbarst, "Proximity" was originally published in the anthology *Alchemy and Miracles: Nature Woven Into Words* (Gilbert and Hall Press, Canada, 2023). Printed with permission of the author.

Clare Bercot Zwerling, "1945" was first published in *Poetry South, Issue 12* (2020). Printed with permission of the author.

Acknowledgements

Many thanks to all the poets and lovers of poetry who jumped in to help this project become a reality. I am grateful to Cynthia Frank of QED Press for all the early support and time offered to explain the intricacies of the publishing world and encourage me to take on this anthology. Likewise, the knowledge and support offered from Wild Ocean Press publisher, Robert Yoder, was invaluable in navigating all that is needed to transform a manuscript into a book.

I have much appreciation for M.L. Mackie's initial vision to gather poems of Mendocino women into the anthology, *Wood, Water, Air and Fire*, and grateful for the experience of being a contributing editor on that book, which inspired me to publish *Spirit of Place* twenty-seven years later.

Many thanks to Mark and Merle Ruedrich for providing the project with a wonderful venue, The Sequoia Room at North Coast Brewery for a benefit reading, and their on-going support of the poetry community over the years. A shout out to the Grace Hudson Museum in Ukiah for their support and for the poets who gave their time and poetry to read at county-wide benefits.

I was fortunate to have a great group of editors who spent hours reading poems and sharing their ideas and visions for the book, Maureen Eppstein, Karen Lewis, blake more, Kate Dougherty and Georgina Marie Guardado. Their help and support was invaluable.

Thanks to our proof-readers, Kathleen Alexander, Barbara Barkovich, Henri Bensussen, Kate Dougherty and Georgina Marie Guardado, to our interior layout designer, Maureen Eppstein, and to Solange Roberdeau for cover art and design. Thanks also to Amanda Cruise for sharing her insights and skills in marketing and trouble-shooting. Much appreciation to Alyssum Wier, Executive Director of the Arts Council of Mendocino County for support and guidance.

Finally, I am grateful to Angela Knox, Wendy and Don Roberts, David and Diana Eppstein, and other donors who so generously funded our publication costs.

— Devreaux Baker

www.ingramcontent.com/pod-product-compliance
Lightning Source LLC
Chambersburg PA
CBHW021107130626
46554CB00002B/566